Thomas S. Lyons, Roger E. Hamlin, and Amaı

Using Entrepreneurship and Social Innovatic

Thomas S. Lyons,
Roger E. Hamlin, and Amanda Hamlin

Using Entrepreneurship and Social Innovation to Mitigate Wealth Inequality

—

ISBN 978-1-5474-1661-5
e-ISBN (PDF) 978-1-5474-0046-1
e-ISBN (EPUB) 978-1-5474-0048-5

Library of Congress Control Number: 2018956918

Bibliographic information published by the Deutsche Nationalbibliothek
The Deutsche Nationalbibliothek lists this publication in the Deutsche Nationalbibliografie;
detailed bibliographic data are available on the Internet at http://dnb.dnb.de.

© 2018 Thomas S. Lyons, Roger E. Hamlin, and Amanda Hamlin
Published by Walter de Gruyter Inc., Boston/Berlin
Printing and binding: CPI books GmbH, Leck
Typesetting: MacPS, LLC, Carmel

www.degruyter.com

About De|G PRESS

Five Stars as a Rule

De|G PRESS, the startup born out of one of the world's most venerable publishers, De Gruyter, promises to bring you an unbiased, valuable, and meticulously edited work on important topics in the fields of business, information technology, computing, engineering, and mathematics. By selecting the finest authors to present, without bias, information necessary for their chosen topic *for professionals*, in the depth you would hope for, we wish to satisfy your needs and earn our five-star ranking.

In keeping with these principles, the books you read from De|G PRESS will be practical, efficient and, if we have done our job right, yield many returns on their price.

We invite businesses to order our books in bulk in print or electronic form as a best solution to meeting the learning needs of your organization, or parts of your organization, in a most cost-effective manner.

There is no better way to learn about a subject in depth than from a book that is efficient, clear, well organized, and information rich. A great book can provide life-changing knowledge. We hope that with De|G PRESS books you will find that to be the case.

DOI 10.1515/9781547400461-202

Acknowledgments

Writing a book is a complex undertaking that requires the collaborative efforts and insights of many people to bring it to fruition. This book is no exception, and we have many people to thank for their contributions. First, we want to convey our gratitude to Jeffrey Pepper of De|G PRESS, our editor, and his assistant Jaya Dalal for their professionalism and support. Thank you for giving us this opportunity to express ourselves and to do so as effectively as possible. We want to thank Monica Dean of Smith College and Edward Rogoff of Long Island University for allowing us to share the story of Competition THRIVE in Chapter 5. Our sincere gratitude to Marvin Austin for taking the time to talk with us about The West Side Business Xcelerator in Chicago. Thanks, too, to the hardworking men and women of the MSU Product Center for the information used in Chapter 7. We also would like to thank Professor Jerzy Cieslik and his team at Kozminski University in Warsaw, Poland, for generously providing us with detailed information and insightful observations about the Warsaw Entrepreneurship Forum discussed in Chapter 8. Our gratitude goes out to our respective institutions—Michigan State University and Oakton College—for their support. We thank our families and friends for their encouragement throughout the process of writing this book. Finally, we salute all the entrepreneurs—civic, commercial, and social—whose creative and innovative work brings all of us a better life and continued hope for the future.

Thomas S. Lyons
Roger E. Hamlin
Amanda R. Hamlin

DOI 10.1515/9781547400461-203

About the Authors

Thomas S. Lyons, Ph.D. is Professor of Agricultural, Food and Resource Economics and Director of the MSU Product Center, Food-Ag-Bio at Michigan State University, which is an organization that supports entrepreneurship in the food, agriculture, and natural resources sectors of the Michigan economy. His research specializations are entrepreneur skill development, the relationship between entrepreneurship and community economic development, and social entrepreneurship. He is the co-author of thirteen books and numerous articles and papers on these subjects, and has edited a three-volume set on social entrepreneurship (*Social Entrepreneurship: How Businesses Can Transform Society*, 2012). His book *Understanding Social Entrepreneurship*, co-authored with Dr. Jill Kickul, is the leading textbook on this subject, used at over eighty universities around the world. In 2011, Dr. Lyons received the Ted K. Bradshaw Outstanding Research Award from the Community Development Society. Lyons has been the holder of two endowed professorships: the Fifth Third Bank Professor in Community Development at the University of Louisville and the Lawrence N. Field Family Chair in Entrepreneurship at Baruch College, City University of New York. He is a practicing entrepreneur, who has co-founded two companies. He holds a doctorate in urban and regional planning from the University of Michigan, Ann Arbor.

Roger E. Hamlin, Ph.D. is Professor Emeritus of Michigan State University, Associate Dean for International Affairs at Babes-Bolyai University and President of Proaction Institute Incorporated, a non-profit economic research and publication organization. He has directed two university urban planning programs, been deputy director of the Institute for Public Policy and Social Research at Michigan State, directed many university projects and has worked for the New York Offices of Planning Services and Senate. Hamlin has been a visiting professor at Tokyo Science University and an Investment Programmer with the Ministry of Housing and Urban Development in Chile. He has authored or co-authored fourteen books on various aspects of local economic development and numerous chapters and articles. He has been an advisor to the prime minister of Romania and has been a consultant to many corporations and institutions in various countries. Dr. Hamlin has lived in Europe, Asia and Latin America and has worked to build local economic development capacity all over the world. His masters and Ph.D. degrees are from the Maxwell School at Syracuse University in Economics, Public Policy and Planning. His undergraduate degree in Economics is from Hamilton College in New York.

DOI 10.1515/9781547400461-204

Amanda R. Hamlin earned a dual degree in Creative Writing and Literature from Carnegie Mellon University in Pittsburgh, a master's degree from Loyola University in Chicago, and a second masters from the University of Illinois ION (Illinois Online Network) Center. She is currently a Ph.D. candidate at Babes-Bolyai University. She has taught scientific writing and introductory writing and English as a Second Language at Loyola University, Chicago City Colleges, Michigan State University English Language Center, Babes-Bolyai University, and the Oakton Community College, for over twelve years. Her previous research publications relate to local strategic planning and local "Innovation City" research parks around the world.

About the Series Editor

Alexandra Reed Lajoux is Series Editor for De|G PRESS, a division of Walter De Gruyter, Inc. The series has an emphasis on governance, corporate leadership, and sustainability. Dr. Lajoux is chief knowledge officer emeritus (CKO) at the National Association of Corporate Directors (NACD) and founding principal of Capital Expert Services, LLC (CapEx), a global consultancy providing expert witnesses for legal cases. She has served as editor of *Directors & Boards, Mergers & Acquisitions, Export Today,* and *Director's Monthly*, and has coauthored a series of books on M&A for McGraw-Hill, including *The Art of M&A* and eight spin-off titles on strategy, valuation, financing, structuring, due diligence, integration, bank M&A, and distressed M&A. For Bloomberg/Wiley, she coauthored *Corporate Valuation for Portfolio Investment* with Robert A. G. Monks. Dr. Lajoux serves on the advisory board of Campaigns and Elections, and is a Fellow of the Caux Round Table for Moral Capitalism. She holds a B.A. from Bennington College, a Ph.D. from Princeton University, and an M.B.A. from Loyola University in Maryland. She is an associate member of the American Bar Association and is certified as a Competent Communicator by Toastmasters International.

DOI 10.1515/9781547400461-205

Contents

Introduction

This is a book about methods that can be used to help solve a problem that faces most societies in the world: the growing gap between the "haves" and the "have nots." This is one of humankind's "wicked" social problems. Wicked because of its current and potential deleterious effects on societal health and stability and because it seems intractable. One answer to the question of how to solve the problem is in a word, *entrepreneurship*. That is, giving those who have limited options financially (because of geography or social conditions) opportunities to create their own businesses, generate financial wealth for themselves and their families, and hire more people like themselves. This requires communities to think and act entrepreneurially in support of increased entrepreneurship activity. It involves entrepreneurs serving other entrepreneurs.

Without the ability to ensure a solution's success, governments cannot solve the inequity problem because they lack innovative approaches and the consistent political will to implement them. Traditional business does not see a realistic solution to this problem and so will not solve it in large part because the profit incentive is not clear to them and partly because they are not aware of successful plans that will work. This means that to this point in history, our two principal societal institutions, throughout most of the world, have been incapable of addressing wealth inequality. It is time to change that in a more meaningful way. It is time to explore new solutions that bring government, businesses, and other societal stakeholders together in support of an approach that can work.

While we are not believers in panaceas, we do think that entrepreneurs are a group able and willing to help us mitigate the wealth inequality problem by encouraging the addition of more entrepreneurs and by creating opportunities for those entrepreneurs to succeed. Entrepreneurs can set the example for those corporations and governments to make them understand the lost opportunity and the immense cost of the status quo. Entrepreneurs who pursue social missions (such as addressing wealth inequality)—known as "social entrepreneurs"—use markets to tackle social problems. They also employ the skills, tools, techniques, processes, and mindset of commercial entrepreneurship to achieve their goals (Kickul & Lyons, 2016). They tend to eschew ideology (Bornstein, 2007); relying instead upon understanding and moral judgment as their driving forces (Mair & Noboa, 2006). They believe in their own self-efficacy and the support of their networks (Mair & Noboa, 2006). They seek to create social value before economic value (Dees, 1998). While they must recognize the need to respect the context within which they operate (Cho, 2006), these characteristics allow them to operate more independently from the constraints that limit others. By generating more entrepreneurs who most naturally have that spirit, a multiplier effect is

DOI 10.1515/9781547400461-207

established, and more and more entrepreneurs can be generated to turn around distressed areas.

Before we tackle how entrepreneurship can be used as an effective force in providing significantly better incomes and more wealth, it is essential to establish some background. What is wealth inequality? How big a problem is it? Why should society care about its solution? These are the questions examined in Chapter 1.

In Chapter 2, we look at the difference between growth and development and why that distinction is crucial to effectively addressing wealth inequality. We also investigate the importance of the link between economic development and community.

Chapter 3 studies the recent interest in entrepreneurship and the role of entrepreneurship-focused economic development in strengthening the link between economic development and community. It also explores the upsurge in social entrepreneurship activities in the past couple of decades. What are the implications of these developments for mitigating wealth inequality?

An entrepreneurship-driven strategy for economic development that addresses wealth inequality must be intentional, focused on true entrepreneurship and not merely self-employment, and dedicated to *developing* entrepreneurs. It must engage at two levels: that of the individual entrepreneurs and that of the nonprofit, private, or public organizations that support the entrepreneur, which is the level at which social entrepreneurship takes place. Chapter 4 provides the details of such a strategy.

At this point, the conceptual foundation is laid, and the book offers a set of international examples of ways in which entrepreneurship is, or has been, used as a tool for dealing with wealth inequality. Chapter 5 chronicles the innovative Competition THRIVE program in New York City, which involved a partnership between city government, a private foundation, and an institution of higher education. The goal was to mitigate poverty in city neighborhoods by fostering immigrant entrepreneurship, but rather than directly support the activities of immigrant entrepreneurs, Competition THRIVE encourages innovation among the support organizations that serve these entrepreneurs in a unique and impactful way.

Entrepreneurship helps individuals, families, and communities to create wealth. However, this only happens when entrepreneurs can move their businesses past the early life cycle stages and into a place of growth. A Chicago NGO, Bethel New Life, recognized this and created a program, called the Westside Xcelerator, which sought to help low-income entrepreneurs to capture markets outside of their neighborhoods and grow their ventures. While this effort was ultimately unsuccessful, the recounting of this story in Chapter 6 offers valuable insights into the challenges inherent in efforts to narrow the wealth gap.

Chapter 7 examines the case of the Michigan State University Product Center Food-Ag-Bio. The Product Center has developed a statewide network of counselors who assist agricultural and food product entrepreneurs and connect them to the considerable resources of the university as these entrepreneurs start and grow their businesses. By taking a "big tent" approach to entrepreneurship, this program has empowered numerous individuals from economically disadvantaged backgrounds to create wealth for themselves and their families through entrepreneurship in contexts ranging from sparsely populated rural counties in the Upper Peninsula of Michigan to Detroit.

Chapter 8 discusses a partnership between city government and a private university that created an entrepreneur network in each of several pilot districts of Warsaw, Poland. These networks fostered mutual support and learning among the entrepreneurs, as the founding partners intentionally played a catalytic role. This example offers additional insights as to how this work is modified in an economy that is transitioning from communism to capitalism.

The lumber industry in the Zapotec village of Ixtlan benefits the members of the community in various ways, including providing funds to help them start their own businesses, reducing conditions of poverty, providing skill and management/leadership training, supporting local businesses by using local inputs, and encouraging the participation of women in the local government. The rural Irish pub culture is beneficial to local communities both socially and economically by providing a social meeting place and a space for business networking, offering work experience and job training for young people, and supporting businesses by buying local. However, both these approaches to social entrepreneurship/innovation are facing challenges from the outside/modern world that threaten their existence. Chapter 9 describes and compares these two examples of community entrepreneurship.

Chapter 10 looks at entrepreneurship among indigenous people in Alaska and Arizona. The State of Alaska has chosen to manage the rights of Native people by organizing each tribe or sub-tribe into its own corporation. The effects of this have been both positive and negative. These Alaskan Native Corporations (ANCs) are both similar to and different from benefit corporations, which is a legal structure available to non-Natives for forming social enterprises. On the reservations of the Apache Tribe in Arizona, economic and social conditions are poor. Residents are plagued by unemployment, low self-esteem, drug abuse, and poor school attendance. An attempt is being made to address this through the creation of an entrepreneurship training program, which concentrates on creating businesses that focus on community interaction and benefit. In both cases, the business entities formed have a mission of serving the economic and social needs of the community, in keeping with Native values. This raises an interesting counterpoint to the more Western cultural orientation of this book, which comes from the perspective that society needs to reframe its thinking about business from an individual to a community endeavor. Clearly, there are exceptions to this view that can and should be perpetuated. The lesson here is that while the idea that economic inequality can be addressed through entrepreneurship may be universal, the way in which this is manifested must be culturally specific.

We close in Chapter 11 by arguing that while these examples are positive steps along the path to responsible, entrepreneurship-focused economic development that address wealth inequality, they, alone, are not enough to transform their respective economies. This chapter explores systemic approaches that create the synergy to transform, increasingly referred to as "entrepreneurial ecosystems."

With this book, it is our intention to shed some light on the important problem of wealth inequality and to offer a possible solution, in an objective way. We aim to take the reader on a journey of discovery that examines the problem and its impacts and explores the potentials and limitations of entrepreneurship as a strategy for its mitigation.

References

Bornstein, D. (2007). *How to change the world: Social entrepreneurs and the power of new ideas*. Oxford, UK: Oxford University Press.

Cho, A.H. (2006). Politics, values and social entrepreneurship: A critical appraisal. In J. Mair, J. Robinson, & K. Hockerts (Eds.). *Social entrepreneurship* (pp. 121–136). New York: Palgrave Macmillan.

Dees, J.G. (1998). The meaning of "social entrepreneurship." Palo Alto, CA: Graduate School of Business, Stanford University. Retrieved from http://www.caseatduke.org/documents/dees_sedef.pdf

Kickul, J., & Lyons, T.S. (2016). *Understanding social entrepreneurship: The relentless pursuit of mission in an ever changing world*. New York: Routledge.

Mair, J., & Noboa, E. (2006). Social entrepreneurship: How intentions to create a social venture are formed. In J. Mair, J. Robinson, & K. Hockerts (Eds.). *Social entrepreneurship* (pp. 121–136). New York: Palgrave Macmillan.

Chapter 1
Wealth Inequality: What Is It? Why Do We Care?

To lay the foundation for the various cases that will be presented throughout the book, we must first define what we are talking about. This chapter discusses wealth inequality with data, theory, and conceptual thinking. The next chapter links the concepts with a definition of social entrepreneurship. Without being too hung up on semantics, we need to first clarify the definition or definitions of wealth. The natural tendency is to monetize any concept that has anything to do with economics or finance. Even in the monetary realm, the definition of wealth is not clear. Does it mean monetary income? For people and families to have enough income is important. Most of the goods and services critical for survival and well-being require significant and continuous access to currency in modern societies.

Savings is another measure; being able to tap savings allows for both the purchase of necessities and a greater sense of stability and therefore less anxiety about loss of income in the short run. Net worth is yet another measure. Net worth includes savings and the value of other assets. However, the value of some assets, such as the value of a house, might not be easily tapped without great individual and family disruption. In addition, many people with asset wealth have a large load of liabilities or debts. Their debt burden diminishes the value of their assets and increases pressure driving the need for stable income to make regular payments on debts. It is clear we should look at societal income inequality, asset inequality, and net worth inequality in any study of inequality.

Academics have also tried to put a value on many other forms of wealth such as social capital, friendship networks, security, safety, stability, power, respect, and self-esteem. Essentially every level of Maslow's hierarchy provides fodder for an attempt to define social wealth. Few people consciously put these kinds of things on their personal balance sheet, but they clearly are real and valuable to most people. In fact, many people are willing to expend large amounts of monetary wealth to obtain or attain these forms of social wealth, sometimes successfully and sometimes unsuccessfully.

We should include and perhaps start with an analysis of income, savings, asset, and net worth inequality. Then we will look at various forms of social inequality.

We must also give some attention to the word "inequality." While its definition seems more obvious, it can take many forms, with many distinct consequences. Is having very few individuals on the top of a pyramid according to some measure, with nearly everyone else at an equal level near the bottom, considered equality or inequality? What if the pyramid was equally distributed from top to bottom with a substantial distance from top to bottom? Is that greater or less

DOI 10.1515/9781547400461-001

inequality than the first case? What are the economic, social and political effects of each on a community or society?

In Figure 1.1, the graph of the distribution of people and households (y-axis) in various income categories (x-axis) is generally a modified bell curve with a tail in the direction of upper income. This means that a majority of people cluster around a mean and median income level with a small number of people at ultra-high income. Since 1971, the high-income tail shown in Figure 1.1 has increased in length as the lump of the curve has flattened. Income of the middle class has changed little, adjusted for inflation, since 1980. This means that income disparities have increased.

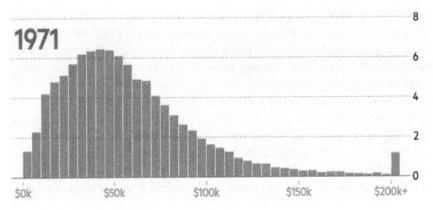

Source: FT graphic Alan Smith, Pew Research Center

Figure 1.1: Household Income in 2014 Dollars: The Percentage of Adults in Each Income Category

In Figure 1.2, the average annual income of individuals in two percentile categories are compared. The line at the bottom represents the average annual income of people who are in the bottom 90 percent of income earned. This line indicates a slow but steady progression of average annual income. The other line represents the average annual income of people in the first percentile (top 1 percent) of income earned. This line also shows a fairly steady progression from the beginning of the chart until 1986 with the exception of a rapid rise just before the great depression and a rapid temporary fall during the depression. In about 1986, the line begins to rise dramatically indicating a rapid increase in the difference between the top 1 percent and the bottom 90 percent, and thus a greater level of income inequality.

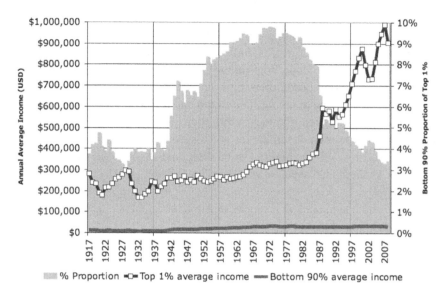

% Proportion ▭ Top 1% average income ━ Bottom 90% average income

Source: Paris School of Economics (http://g-mond.parisschoolofeconomics.eu/topincomes/
Figure 1.2: U.S. Income Distribution, 1917–2008

The U.S. Census Bureau measures and reports several measures of inequality:
- Gini index
- Shares of aggregate household income received by quintiles
- Ratio of income percentiles
- Theil index
- Mean logarithmic deviation of income (MLD)
- Atkinson measure

The Gini index is a statistical measure of income inequality ranging from 0 to 1, with a measure of 1 indicating perfect inequality (one household having all the income and the rest having none) and a measure of 0 indicating perfect equality (all households having an equal share of income). The Theil index and the MLD are similar to the Gini index in that they are single statistics that summarize the dispersion of income across the entire income distribution. The Atkinson measure is useful in determining which end of the income distribution contributed most to inequality.

The share of aggregate household income in the fourth quintile (the lowest 20 to 40 percent) decreased 1.3 percent between 2015 and 2016, while changes in the other quintiles were not statistically significant. The money income Gini index was 0.481 in 2016, not statistically different from 2015. Changes in inequality between 2015 and 2016 were not statistically significant as measured by other indicators such as the Theil index, the MLD, or the Atkinson measure.

Households in the lowest quintile in the United States had incomes of $24,002 or less in 2016. Households in the second quintile had incomes between $24,003 and $45,600, those in the third quintile had incomes between $45,601 and $74,869, and those in the fourth quintile had incomes between $74,870 and $121,018. Households in the highest quintile had incomes of $121,019 or more. The top 5 percent of households in the income distribution had incomes of $225,252 or more. World wealth inequality can be discussed in the same way; although, the dollar denominated absolute values are much lower and the inequality much larger.

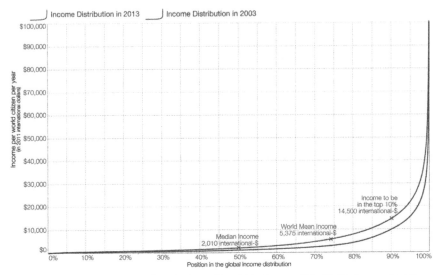

Source: Thomas Hellebrandt and Paolo Mauro (2015) The Future of Worldwide Income Distribution, working paper. The data visualization is available at OurWorldData.org. See below for discussion.

Figure 1.3: Global Income Distribution by Percentile: Comparison of 2003 to 2013.

The Gini index is often used to measure global income inequality. The United Nations University World Income Inequality Database also measures income inequality by country and over time. According to the Gini index, inequality is the greatest in the poorest countries and was greater in the past than it is today.

However, this does not mean that income inequality does not exist in the modern developed world. No matter what measure is used, income inequality is a reality and evidence suggests it is on the rise. Historical trends in the United

States, as shown in Figure 1.2, show a pattern of persistent income-inequality during both periods of economic growth and economic stagnation.

> For a period of roughly 30 years, beginning at the end of World War II and extending through the early 1970s, the United States boasted a robust middle class and relatively low levels of income inequality. But, for the last four decades, income and wealth inequality have been rising precipitously. Currently, the top 10 per cent of American earners take in roughly 49.9 per cent of total income, a level of income concentration almost unparalleled in American history... The income share of the top 1 per cent increased from 20.1 per cent in 2013 to 21.2 per cent in 2014. While rich and poor alike lost financial ground during the Great Recession of 2008, higher earners have regained their footing, while the average Joe (or Josephine) lag behind. From 2009–2014, the incomes of the top 1 per cent grew by 27.1 per cent, while the income of the bottom 99 per cent grew by only 4.3 per cent. Essentially, the top 1 per cent captured 58 per cent of the income gains in the five years post-2008 when the economy was stabilizing. (Waldman, 2017: 24)

These trends can be seen in a variety of measures of wealth, such as "ratios between CEO pay and the salary of an average worker. Reports from union databases estimate the multiplicand to be roughly 331:1, growing from 42:1 in 1980, to 107:1 in 1990, before increasing to its current dizzying levels" (Waldman, 2017: 25), as well as measures of net worth as opposed to raw income. Further, "More recent estimates based on tax records suggest that the top 1 per cent of households own close to 42 per cent of total wealth (nearly double the wealth held by the bottom 20 per cent) and that wealth inequality continues to accelerate driven largely by spectacular increases garnered by the top 0.01 per cent" (Waldman, 2017: 26).

These trends have continued as the economy has recovered from the recession when the "biggest increases continued to flow to higher-income workers. Median income rose 3 percent to $16,000 for the lowest percentile of households and 9% for the top group with median earnings of $251,000. That expanded the nation's income divide. From 2013 to 2016, the share of income going to the top 1% of families climbed to 23.8% from 20.3% The portion going to the bottom 90% slipped from about 54% to 50%" (Davidson, 2017: 1). With a similar growth in wealth inequality in net worth where "The richest households reaped the biggest gains as the median net worth for the top percentile rose 24% to $2.4 million. There was barely any increase for the bottom group with median net worth of $200. As a result, the share of wealth held by the top 1% of households rose to 38.6% from 36.3% over the three-year period. The portion controlled by the bottom 90% has been falling for decades—from 33.2% in 1989 to 22.8%" in 2016 (Davidson, 2017: 1).

In addition, the issue is not confined to the United States alone. Rather, "The trend toward wealth and income inequality is global in nature. Today, seven out of 10 people live in countries where inequality today is greater than it was 30 years ago. Moreover, in most countries around the world, inequality is increasing at ever accelerating rates. According to data compiled by Oxfam International, the wealthiest 1 per cent command more of the world's wealth than the rest of the population combined. And, in 2015, just 62 individuals had the same wealth as 3.6 billion people comprising the bottom 50 per cent of earners round the globe" (Waldman, 2017: 26). All the above make a strong case for the persistence and even the growth of wealth inequality, over time, across a variety of measures, and around the globe. The graph in Figure 1.3 indicates the average annual income (y-axis) of each percentile of the world population (x-axis). The rapid up swing of the graph on the right side indicates the rapid increase in income as one moves to the top income percentiles. More significantly, the graph shows the shift from 2003 to 2013, with the line below indicating the distribution in 2003 and the line slightly above it showing the distribution in 2013. The upward shift over time, particularly on the right side of the graph indicates a greater concentration of income in the upper percentile groups worldwide.

Why Do We Care?

Some argue that income inequality is not in itself a problem. Some people have success and some do not. The argument is both a fairness argument and an economic postulate. Some claim that income inequality creates an incentive system for people to aspire to do better. This incentivizes hard work, frugality, and innovation. The standard macro-economic model says that economic growth can not take place unless a society can produce a surplus, that is, more than is needed to subsist, and that surplus is saved, that is, not consumed. Economic growth happens when that savings is translated into investment. Investment means channeling saved time and talent into anything that increases efficiencies and therefore increases the potential surplus. Investment can include building new factories, making better machines, training the workforce, and educating the population.

One argument concerning income inequality is that people residing on the high-income right tail of the income distribution graph have more disposable income, which produces more saving and the translation of savings into investment. This is sometimes called a supply-side argument since investments increase the quality and quantity of the factors of production. Whether this happens is a matter of debate, and some would argue that the supply side could be looked at in another way. One can argue that a society with a sophisticated financial intermediary system can get more investment out of a less unequal income distribution. Does society get more savings and investment out of several hundred million middle-class households putting money into IRAs, 401(k)s, 403(b)s, and other annuities than society receives out of a few billionaires investing directly? In addition, which type of investment produces greater efficiency in the long run? These are the arguments that confront one another in pure macroeconomic terms.

The other way to look at macroeconomics is from the demand side. A high demand or mass market for goods and services will induce investors and entrepreneurs to invest in factors of production and to invest to meet the population's needs. A society with a large middle class is most effective in generating that mass market. Some would claim that the power of a large and broad middle class accounts for much of United States' economic success during the twentieth century. Arguments related to saving inequality and net worth inequality follow along the same lines.

In addition, some economists have argued that wealth inequality can cause unstable economies, increase the likelihood of financial crisis, and make it difficult for an economy to sustain growth over the long term. Their studies have indicated that "increasing the length of growth spells, rather than just getting growth going, is critical to achieving income gains over the long term and countries with more equal income distributions tend to have significantly longer growth spells" and reducing wealth inequality by 10 percent can increase the length of economic growth cycles by as much as 50 percent (Berg & Ostry, 2017: 88). Wealth inequality creates economic instability that leads "high-income individuals to save, low-income individuals to sustain consumption through borrowing, and financial institutions and regulators to encourage the process" (Berg & Ostry, 2017: 793). Specifically, "Poor people may not have the means to finance their education. An equal distribution of income could thus increase investment in human capital and hence growth... Income inequality may increase the risk of political instability, and the resulting uncertainty could reduce incentives to invest and hence impair growth" and this may be exacerbated as the haves and have nots try to battle it out in the political arena to impact policy on things like taxes and health insurance to protect their own interest (Berg & Ostry, 2017: 795). The above evidence suggests that mitigation of income inequality has the potential to benefit the economy of an area and, therefore, all residents of the area, regardless of where they fall on the wealth scale.

Poverty

In addition to the above, the increase in and concentration of poverty has the potential to introduce a variety of social and economic concerns that will certainly affect the individuals living in poverty but also has the potential to affect the wider society as well. Although the poverty line is somewhat arbitrary and differs somewhat by program or agency, the assumption is that it represents a level of income below which people and families suffer various forms of deprivation, including poor housing, poor health, low education, family instability, and lack of transportation, to name a few. Ultimately important is that many of the deprivations of poverty reduce one's ability to be independent, to rise out of poverty, and to make contributions to society. In addition to the personal tragedies, the real danger here is that poverty can become self-perpetuating and exacerbate income inequality over time. Thus, it is defined as a "wicked problem."

Some claim that poverty causes societal problems and expense as well. Poverty might make public health more fragile, for example, creating an environment in which disease can spread more easily. Studies show that this gap has widened rather than improved with time as "Thirty years ago, life expectancy in the United States was five years longer for the upper quintile of income than for the lowest quintile. Today, that difference is 12 years for men and 14 years for women. Worse yet, life spans have not improved for lower-income people, and marginal loss of longevity has occurred for women" (Vega & Sribney, 2017: 1606). However, "It is not income status per se that predisposes to disease; rather, income inequality creates a propensity to disease pathways over the course of human development through environmental exposures and learned behavior in specific social contexts." For example, "Low-income obese persons are progressing to dysfunction much more rapidly than high-income people. In their age of onset trajectory to deficits in activities of daily living, healthy-weight persons who are low income are similar to extremely obese higher-income persons rather than to healthy-weight higher-income persons. These findings suggest that total disease burden borne by people at the lower end of income distribution is greater irrespective of any specific medical condition" (Vega & Sribney, 2017: 1606). These health discrepancies are due, not only to the environment in which poor people live but also to their very unequal access to medical care. The stereotype of those in poverty being uninsured carries some truth in that 17 percent of the population was uninsured prior to the Affordable Care Act, but this number only dropped to 8.8 percent after the Act was instituted (Christopher et al., 2018).

However, the link between the poor and lack of health care is more complex than simply people living in abject poverty who can not afford insurance at all. Even if one can afford to pay a basic insurance premium, out of pocket costs can still make a significant impact on the quality of life since "As copayments and deductibles have risen, insured families' out-of-pocket costs for care have increased over the past decade, outstripping income gains. At present, medical bills are the most common type of debt sent to collection agencies," specifically "The proportion of privately insured employees whose individual coverage carries an annual deductible of $2000 or more has increased 6-fold since 2006" (Christopher et al., 2018: 352). The ramifications of this increase in terms of the growth of poverty are significant.

> In 2013, medical outlays lowered the median income (calculated after subtracting medical expenditures) for the poorest decile by 49.2% and by 10.7% for the next poorest group versus 2.5% for the wealthiest decile, a markedly regressive pattern. This unequal pattern improved only slightly in 2014. In that year, medical outlays lowered median income in the lowest income decile by 47.6% versus 2.7% in the top decile. For those in the top 1.0% of income, medical outlays decreased income by only 1.3%. In 2014, 9.28 million Americans whose incomes before their medical outlays were above poverty were pushed into near poverty (150% of FPL [Federal Poverty Level]) when medical outlays were subtracted from their family incomes. Similarly, 7.013 million were lowered into poverty (below 100% of the FPL), and for 3.946 million, medical outlays reduced their incomes into the extreme poverty range (below 50% of the FPL). (Christopher et al., 2018: 354)

Further, it can be argued that issues with discrepancies in health care exist because the system itself fails to take the reality of wealth inequality into account: "Because patient-paid costs and private insurance premiums are seldom indexed to income, they consume a larger share of income of low- versus high-income individuals. For example, whereas paying $5000 for premiums and copayments is 1% of income for an executive making $500,000, it is 10% of income for a teacher earning $50,000. Although the same could be said about $5000 spent on items such as vehicles or food, individuals (especially those with serious or chronic illnesses, who account for most medical spending) have little discretion about their medical outlays" (Christopher et al., 2018: 353). In addition to the fact that the cost of private insurance is rising, there has also been an increase in the cost of Medicaid for low-income individuals, an increase in that it was formerly free. Now, however, "Centers for Medicare & Medicaid Services have allowed several states to impose cost sharing on Medicaid recipients, reversing a long-standing rule against such policies. For instance, Indiana received a waiver allowing it to require $10 monthly payments from Medicaid recipients and to revoke or downgrade coverage for those who miss a payment. This policy, designed by the current Centers for Medicare & Medicaid Services administrator, has resulted in lost or downgraded coverage for more than half of enrollees" (Christopher et al., 2018: 354). The rising cost of health insurance on every front means that the health concerns associated with wealth inequality are likely to continue or increase in the near future.

In addition to such health issues, poverty can also decrease quality of life by increasing crime rates, which places a burden on the entire criminal justice system from courts to prisons to the cost of police protection. Crime can also increase the cost of production of products and services by adding to the security needs of firms. The relationship between poverty and crime is complex. On the most basic level, lack of a legal means to provide enough income can lead to the use of illegal means to make up the difference. This is shown in a study in which crime rose in cycles that correlated with the area's public assistance grants, with the high point of crime occurring when people's funds are likely to be lowest and, in another study, where prisoners that were given financial assistance on release were less likely to repeat offend in the near future (Sharkey et al., 2016). However, there is more at work in the relationship between poverty and crime than mere economic necessity. Research has also indicated that the frustrations caused by pronounced wealth inequality may also lead to increased crime by driving people to take their aggression out on others, especially those they perceive as economically more privileged (Greitemeyer & Sagioglou, 2017).

In addition to theories about individual poverty and crime, there is also evidence of links between crime and community poverty. In a poor community, people are more likely to see others who commit crimes out of economic necessity who then serve as models for more crimes, while they are simultaneously less likely to see models of successfully employed individuals. In addition, the lack of vigilance against crime by both police and other community members may also make crime appear more viable in these areas (Sharkey et al., 2016). These causes also point to important emotional ramifications of poverty and associated crime including the reduction of trust between individuals, between individuals and institutions, and between individuals and government. Trust is a critical lubricant of every economic and social interaction. A lower level of trust in society means that every transaction between societal participants is slower and more expensive. A low trust society means more paper work, more need for oversight and secondary checks, and more effort needed to create clear communication. Ultimately, it means higher personal discount rates, which means that people put less faith in the future and are less willing to take risks with future payoff. Long-term capital assets such as homes, factories and bridges and highways become less valuable and attract less long-term investment. Ultimately, higher real interest rates reflect a less trusting society.

Poverty can also cause geographic agglomeration problems. Poverty populations often live in separate enclaves from the rest of society, partly because the rest of society shuns poorer people and partly because this is where they can find the economic and social support they need for survival. Lower income ghettos often mean pockets of lower quality public services such as schools because poverty populations do not have the political power needed to demand top quality services. Poverty ghettos also often lack high quality business services because businesses feel that operating there is more costly. Food deserts, for example, have been an issue in many large U.S. cities, where supermarket chains do not want to build, forcing the local population to buy food that is more expensive from convenience grocers and/or eat less nutritious and more expensive fast food, because it is the only thing available.

A food desert is defined as "a geographical concept designed to capture the persistent retail gaps that exist in food provisioning in poor and underserved neighborhoods typically in inner cities, but also in rural communities. Food deserts are described as areas devoid of supermarkets, areas with limited access to affordable and nutritious food, or areas with limited access to food, which also suffer from deprivation and social exclusion" (Howerton & Trauger, 2017: 746) and the Economic Research Service of the United States Department of Agriculture defines them as "low-income census tracts where at least 33%, or 500 residents, have limited access to a supermarket or large grocery store" (Santorelli & Okeke, 2017: 993). In these measures, limited access is usually defined as within one mile or less. Statistics indicate that over twenty-five million people or 14 percent of the population are adversely affected by these kinds of food shortages. Because most of the food accessible in food deserts is fast food or low quality and fresh produce is particularly hard to come by, this compounds the problem of lower quality of health for poor people caused by the discrepancies in health insurance described above. In addition, the lack of mobility for poor people caused by transit limitations, as shown in the following paragraphs, renders food deserts even more problematic, as it makes poor people incapable of accessing resources, including quality food, outside of their own, often poorly developed neighborhoods (Howerton & Trauger, 2017).

Further, geographic agglomeration of poverty often means that lower income people have difficulty getting to the places they need. The people needing jobs often have trouble accessing employers, for example. As factories need greater amounts of horizontal space they tend to move to suburban locations far from lower-income neighborhoods. If served by public transportation, these jobs might require a multi-hour commute by transit dependent people. Often governmental offices and courts, post offices, recycling sites, and welfare services are difficult to access by public transit. The concept of this discrepancy between where people live and where jobs are available is known as the spatial mismatch hypothesis which, in its original form Lingqian Hu defines as follows "1) housing market segregation has limited the housing choices of blacks and constrained them in the inner cities; 2) suburbanization of employment—especially low-skill and low-wage jobs—has reduced the number of suitable jobs for blacks living in the inner city; and 3) blacks living in the inner city do not have affordable or efficient transportation to travel to suburban jobs" (Hu, 2015: 33).

Although there are some variations, the spatial mismatch hypothesis still provides valuable insight regarding the barriers to job acquisition facing poor and minority city dwellers. Some such variations include the skill mismatch hypothesis, which argues that "cities have plenty of job opportunities, but these jobs require high-level skills that many inner-city job seekers do not have" and the information mismatch hypothesis which claims "living in segregated inner-city neighborhoods limits the social contacts of poor job seekers with the mainstream society that could supply relevant information about job openings" (Hu, 2015: 34). However, these alternative theories continue to reinforce the relationship between poverty, geographic isolation, and lack of access to quality jobs as they all revolve around the poor being denied the ability to access jobs because they are not able to secure some vital resource (education, skill and training, social connections) often due to the ghettoization of poverty.

A particularly wicked problem associated with income distribution is child poverty. One might think that this is not an issue in a wealthy country like the United States. Children International estimates that 1 in 7 children are born into poverty in the United States, and the Urban Institute estimates that nearly 40 percent of children spend at least one year in poverty during their childhood (Children International, 2018). Poor children are more likely to experience hunger, an experience with lifelong implications. More than six million children die every year worldwide from malnutrition. However, in the United States, childhood obesity is a more visible concern (though obesity does not preclude malnutrition) and like malnutrition it is an issue in which economic status plays a significant role. As stated above, those who live in poverty are more likely to experience health problems for a variety of reasons and this is not different for children as can be seen in the following evidence.

> The prevalence of obesity among boys living in households with income at or above 350% of the poverty level is 11.9%, while 21.1% of those who live below 130% of the poverty level are obese. Among girls, 12.0% of those with income at or above 350% of the poverty level are obese while 19.3% of those with income below 130% of the poverty level are obese... Of the approximately 12 million children and adolescents who are obese, 24% (almost 3 million) live in households with income at or above 350% of the poverty level, 38% (approximately 4.5 million) have incomes between 130% and 350% of the poverty level, and 38% (approximately 4.5 million) live below 130% of the poverty level. (Ogden et al., 2010: 1)

However, this study shows that the issue of childhood obesity is not linked to poverty alone but also with level of education. "Among boys, 11.8 percent of those living in households where the household head has at least a college degree are obese compared with 21.1 percent of those living in households where the head of the household has less than a high school degree. Among girls, 8.3 percent of children and adolescents in households where the household head has at least a college degree are obese compared with 20.4 percent in households headed by individuals with less than a high school degree" (Ogden et al., 2010: 4). This is very significant because there is also a correlation between level and quality of education and degree of poverty, which, like childhood health and nutritional issues, can create lifelong challenges that make it increasingly difficult for the individual in question to break out of the cycle of poverty.

Education is frequently viewed as the crucial factor in whether a person succeeds in life or not and, while the preceding material regarding issues like geographical and transportation barriers, lack of support networks, and biases against the poor, may call this into question, it still can not be regarded as insignificant in a variety of areas. This discrepancy is known as the achievement gap and reflects the fact that a "vast chasm in academic achievement has long existed along racial and poverty lines. Children of color and from low-income families have, on average, performed worse on virtually all indicators of academic success: standardized test scores, high school graduation rates, and college matriculation rates" (Zhao, 2016: 723). Further, as in the case of child health above, evidence suggests a strong link between parental wealth and educational level and child academic success.

> The merit measured and used to sort individuals are not free from inheritance. IQ scores, SAT, ACT, and all sorts of standardized measures of academic achievement that have been used to determine individuals' access to different educational opportunities and employment opportunities have long been found to be associated with their family background such as social economic status and parental education... Education opportunities and resources for children vary tremendously in the United States. Children of color and low-income families are much more likely to suffer from lower-quality health care and early learning programs than children born into wealthier families. They are much more likely to be subject to violence and unsafe neighborhoods. They attend worse schools and are more likely to have less experienced and lower quality teachers. They are also more likely to be victims of prejudice, racism, and low expectations than their wealthier and nonminority peers. (Zhao, 2016: 725)

This aspect of the achievement gap has a significant impact on future success as can be seen by the fact that in 2016 the median income for college graduates was $92,000 but only $27,000 for those without a college degree, while median net worth was $292,000 for college graduates but only $23,000 to $67,000 for those without college degrees (Davidson, 2017).

Programs, such as No Child Left Behind, intended to address this achievement gap, have proved unsuccessful, perhaps because they are based on the "deficit model" of education in which "children from poor and minority families have been identified as having more deficiencies than their wealthier and Caucasian peers upon entering kindergarten. Their scores in reading and math are much lower when they start school. In order to help them catch up, poor and minority children are given extra dosages of fixing. As a result, many poor children spend their entire school life being helped to catch up but never do" (Zhao, 2016: 726). This is of particular concern because spending catch-up time on basics prevents these children from spending time developing other skills, which are necessary for modern employment because while "the disadvantaged children are put into remediation in reading and math and suffer from the pedagogy of poverty, the more advantaged children are enjoying a much broader curriculum and developing qualities that may be of greater value for admissions to colleges or finding employment. Such skills have generally been referred to as 21st century skills or noncognitive qualities. They have gained more value in the new work place. In other words, even if we fixed the educational achievement gap so disadvantaged children had the similar test scores and even went to college, they face the challenge of credential inflation. When everyone has a college degree, employers look for something else" (Zhao, 2016: 726). This line of reasoning suggests the educational system has, in many ways, not caught up with the changes of modern life and is thus not suited to prepare children for success in the modern world and that, further, the lack of preparation becomes more acute the further down the socioeconomic scale a school or pupil is.

The fact that the poor are undereducated, and this puts them at a lifelong income disadvantage, represents one of the most concerning aspects of wealth inequality—in the way it creates a vicious cycle that is difficult to break out of. In terms of education "Children of the wealthy and dominant social group is[sic] able to produce higher test scores, thanks to their resources, they have access to more rewarding opportunities in life. They then can create better opportunities for their children to have more merit and thus perpetuate their dominance, while the poor and underprivileged can only stay in their cycle of poverty" (Zhao, 2016: 730). But similar statements could be made about almost every aspect of poverty. As the evidence presented thus far shows, the poor have less access to jobs, lack social, financial, and technical resources to better their lives including successful role models, are more likely to be geographically isolated, suffer from crime or ill health, and face a greater financial burden in meeting various costs of living, all of which make it difficult to improve their situation.

Another factor in the cycle of poverty is lack of external assistance in overcoming these kinds of barriers. This can be seen in the trend of welfare reform in accordance with a "workfirst" philosophy, that aims at rapid employment rather than skill building for long-term success, the idea being that employees can learn needed skill on the job and then use these skills to move on to higher paying jobs. However, because these programs operate by moving "disadvantaged populations experiencing a range of individual vulnerabilities (ranging from long-term unemployment, to substance abuse, mental illness, and homelessness) into unsubsidized jobs in the labor market" (Cooney, 2011: 92), it is a reasonable question if the people in these programs will be able to achieve the same level of success as they could in a program that provides "a combination of soft-skill building, hard-skill training, and work experience for individuals at the end of the labor queue" and "provide a first job in a supportive setting with additional skill-building opportunities, ancillary services, and assistance connecting to specific employers in the unsubsidized labor market; an approach that offers work experience and the bridge to a better job" (Cooney, 2011: 98). The concern being that, without the proper support, individuals in these programs will lack the necessary resources to overcome the many barriers locking them into a cycle of poverty.

The next chapter talks about efforts to promote community economic development. It discusses the need to address a broader base of community concerns than just promoting economic growth. Part of that more comprehensive foundation is addressing the complex set of issues associated with the cycle of poverty and increasing wealth inequality, the wicked problems. Chapter 2 sets the stage for a discussion in Chapter 3 on social entrepreneurship as a critical component of a more sustainable form of community economic development. Social entrepreneurs are entrepreneurs who understand that it is in their enlightened self-interest to use some of their revenues and profits to promote the comprehensive development of their community and spread the knowledge, skills, and wealth of their entrepreneurial success. In many cases this can be done in partnerships with many government programs and agencies and many nonprofit organizations. The idea is not just to serve those in poverty but to give a broad base of the population the skills and opportunities to improve their situation by being entrepreneurial, starting new businesses or engaging in other activities by bringing new efforts and innovative ideas to reality. It also involves building a culture of entrepreneurship where people seek to build those skills and abilities in the process of starting new businesses.

As will be discussed, social enterprises provide one possible way of attempting to address the barriers caused by the cycle of poverty and general wealth inequality. Social enterprises can take many forms, as will be seen, but involve private enterprises that work to develop a community by reaching out to many actors, to develop the strengths of the community, and make it a part of their own success. Many of the case studies in this work explore the way that social enterprises disrupt the cycle of poverty by focusing on issues such as skill building, housing and health care, community building, and work environment, rather than simply raw wages. And they examine how the cases succeed (or not) to address the individual challenges faced by the participants. Case studies point out that, when this is done successfully, social entrepreneurship can result in increased success for the social enterprise as well as the individuals within it, which, as explained above, also has the potential to benefit the area in terms of increased economic innovation, growth, and stability.

The following chapters postulate, and perhaps demonstrate, that tapping and developing the skills and abilities of the broader community and guiding them toward the utilization of those skills in entrepreneurial ways can develop local communities. This also can lead to a broader and more robust, sustainable national and global economy, with a dynamic and growing middle class that mitigates the trend toward income and wealth inequality.

References

Berg, A., & Ostry, J. (2017). Inequality and unsustainable growth: Two sides of the same coin? *IMF Economic Review* 65 (4): 792–815.

Brady, D., & Burton, L. (Eds.) (2016). *The Oxford handbook of the social science of poverty.* Oxford, UK: Oxford University Press.

Children International. (2018). Child poverty in the U.S.: Facts and stats about child poverty in the United States. Retrieved from https://www.children.org/global-poverty/global-poverty-facts/facts-about-poverty-in-usa. Accessed August 11, 2018.

Christopher, A., Himmelstien, D., Woolhandler, S., & McCormick, D. (2018). The effects of household medical expenditures on income inequality in the United States. *American Journal of Public Health* 108 (3): 351–354.

Cooney, K. (2011). The business of job creation: An examination of the social enterprise approach of workforce development. *Journal of Poverty* 15: 88–107.

Davidson, P. (9/28/2017). Household income grows, but so does gap. *USA Today.*

Greitmeyer, T., & Sagioglou, C. (2017). Increasing wealth inequality may increase interpersonal hostility: The relationship between personal relative deprivation and aggression. *Journal of Social Psychology* 157 (6): 766–776.

Howerton, G., & Trauger, A. (2017). Oh, honey, don't you know? The social construction of food access in a food desert. *ACME: An International E-Journal for Critical Geographies* 16 (4): 740–760.

Hu, L. (2015). Job accessibility of the poor in Los Angeles: Has suburbanization affected spatial mismatch? *Journal of the American Planning Association* 81 (1): 30–45.

Ogden, C., Lamb, M., Carroll, M., & Flegal, K. (2010). Obesity and socioeconomic status in children and adolescents: United States, 2005–2008. NCHS Data Brief No. 51. Retrieved from https://files.eric.ed.gov/fulltext/ED530165.pdf. Accessed July 18, 2018.

Santorelli, M., & Okeke, J. (2017). Evaluating community measures of healthy food access. *Journal of Community Health* 42 (5): 991–997.

Sharkey, P., Besbris, M., & Friedson, M. (2016). Poverty and crime. In D. Brady & L.M. Burton. *The Oxford handbook of the social science of poverty* (pp. 623–636). Oxford, UK: Oxford University Press.

Vega, W., & Sribney, W. (2017). Growing economic inequality sustains health disparities. *American Journal of Public Health* 107 (10): 1606–1607.

Waldman, E. (2017). Inequality in America and spillover effects on mediation practice: Disputing for the 1 per cent and the 99 per cent. *Law in Context* 35 (1): 24–43.

Zhao, Y. (2016). From deficiency to strength: Shifting the mindset about education inequality. *Journal of Social Issues* 72 (4): 720–739.

Chapter 2
Growth and Development

In this chapter, we look at the difference between growth and development and why that distinction is crucial to effectively addressing wealth inequality. We also investigate the importance of the link between economic development and community. After clarifying definitions, we first look at some ways of thinking about business development that flesh out the distinction between growth and development. Second, we apply those ideas to community economic development. Then we address the link between sophisticated business development and development of the larger community, which leads to a discussion of social entrepreneurship as an approach to address community economic development and wealth inequality.

Definitions

What is the difference between "growth" and "development"? Both of these words are perhaps vague and overused and tend to mean different things in different contexts. Sometimes they are used interchangeably, as if one is a synonym of the other. According to some dictionaries one word is used to define the other. However a difference in connotation, inference, and ultimate implication can be critical to the subject of this book.

First, growth tends to mean an increase or expansion of something. To grow is to rise. In economic terms growth implies an increase in economic activity such as a rise in gross domestic product (GDP) or income. For an individual business, "growth" means an increase in sales, market share, or profit. The result might be an increase in employment and production. The implication is to win by reaching a higher level. While achieving growth is difficult, the objective is simple to understand. An old saying in the business world is that "you either grow or die."

Development, on the other hand, might imply something broader, more complex, and more sophisticated. Development, according to the Onelook Thesaurus that combines many dictionaries (2018) means to become more advanced, more complete. Appropriate synonyms for "development" might be evolution, maturation, progression, formulation, construction, or enhancement. The inferred goal is not just to win in simplistic terms, but to flourish. Rather than just rising, development can mean a broadening of the foundational base, a strengthening of the structure and/or infrastructure, and an increase in potential longevity or sustainability.

DOI 10.1515/9781547400461-002

Therefore, development of a business means more than an increase in sales or profit. It might mean training staff or improving collegiality to have a more effective workforce. Development might mean doing things to improve customer relations or the brand image. It might mean research and development (R&D) to be sure that the firm has viable, up-to-date products and services to offer in the future. It might also mean strengthening relations with the community in which the business is located or which it serves. Investment in some of these endeavors will take time and resources, which might reduce expenditures for increasing sales and market share in the short run but make the business more viable in the long run.

Some of the same distinctions between growth and development can be made at the community level and for society as a whole. As discussed in the previous chapter, mature societies with complex broad-based economies seem to be more resilient than those that have pushed a single growth model based on one product such as natural resources. Economies with the greatest wealth inequality, without a large and varied middle class, often find that growth hits a ceiling without broader development.

Also, as explored in the previous chapter, wealth inequality encompasses more than raw monetary numbers but deals with intangible or harder to measure quantities such as quality of housing, crime rate, and access to health care and education. Therefore, economic growth alone will not address the problem. Only when there is a consciousness shift toward channeling resources toward making things better, rather than just bigger, in other words, toward development as opposed to pure growth, will the issues of wealth inequality be able to be fully addressed.

Also, as will be discussed, as social entrepreneurship systems deepen the participation of community members in the entrepreneurial economy and the economy at large, natural growth can lead to a broader and more sustained wealth development.

Understanding and Promoting Business Development

Economic theories have been around for at least the last several hundred years and, in that time, have undergone many changes from the early "hands off" ideas of laissez-faire and Adam Smith's "invisible hand." Several of the more recent approaches to economics provide useful clues for addressing wealth inequality, such as being oriented toward enabling development as well as growth, setting and gradually working toward goals, looking at economic units as unique and complex structures with individual needs, and enabling all affected stakeholders to have input into relevant economic decisions. Examples of such approaches include strategic planning, learning organizations, systems theory, and complexity science.

As indicated above, investment in some of these endeavors that help businesses avoid being trapped in a short-view, simplistic growth model and lead to a broader development approach will take time and resources. This might reduce expenditures for increasing sales and market share in the short run but make the business more viable in the long run. Strategic planning is one way a business can take this long view and sort out what is sustainable, and what is in its enlightened self-interest. Strategic planning in the modern context got its start in the business world. The Harvard Policy Model of the 1920s is often considered one of the first strategic planning methodologies for private businesses. The model defined "strategy" as a pattern of purposes and policies that acts as a common thread or underlying logic that holds a business together. Strategy weaves a pattern that unites company resources, senior management, and market information (Blackerby, 2003). Over the years, for many firms, strategic planning may have become a more simplistic SWOT exercise than originally contemplated by the Harvard Policy Model. It is often focused more on shorter-term market implications. However, the methodology still demands that an organization start the process by defining what it values, what the organization stands for, and how it wants to be perceived by the rest of the world (Vanravensway, 2015). Values are normative and will differ from one business to another, but it is important for any organization for their value statement to be clear, apparent, and transparent. Mid-range, measurable goals and objectives flow from this statement of values and lead to the actions the organization takes (Hamlin, forthcoming). Values are foundational and help to define the difference between simplistic growth and the sustainable development of the organization (Hintea, 2013).

Another approach to a broader foundation of business development that avoids simplistic growth mentalities is the theory of learning organizations (Senge, 1990). A learning organization "is an organization that has a strong ability to learn, adjust and change in response to new realities. It can alter functions and departments when demanded by changes in the work environment or by poor performance. The distinguishing characteristics of a learning organization include" (Gephart et al., 1996: abstract):

1. A learning culture
2. A spirit of flexibility
3. Respect for experimentation
4. People orientation
5. Continuous learning at the systems level
6. Knowledge generation and sharing

7. Systemic thinking
8. Critical thinking

"To succeed, such an organization must be supported by well-developed core competencies and an attitude that promotes continuous, value-added improvement. It must also be able to renew and revitalize at a basic level" (Gephart et al., 1996: abstract). Such an approach allows an organization to innovate and adapt to change (Gephart et al., 1996).

Due to the rapid changes now occurring in both society and many industries, it can be argued that learning organization principles are critical for businesses of any size. Traditional forms of learning are no longer adequate or enough to enable organizations to develop in the needed ways. Thus, in their article "Management Practices in Learning Organizations," Michael McGill, John Slocum, and David Lei propose that learning organizations need to move away from simple adaptive learning (McGill et al., 1992). Adaptive learning involves reaction to external pressures through the use of precedent—how best to handle a problem based on how people in the past have handled similar problems and how to grow in sales, profit, and market share based on past experience, past trends, and behaviors. We need more generative learning, which would be much closer to what could be described as true innovation (McGill et al., 1992). As in strategic planning, generative learning looks to the future and is anticipatory rather than reactionary but it also does not rely on precedent and focuses on meeting challenges in new and innovative ways, better able to address the current rapidly changing circumstances. Development of an organization implies both kinds of learning as a part of a continuous iterative cycle. The process of building a strategy promotes organizational learning by bringing people and parts of an organization together to focus on the future and on needed innovation. As will be seen, social enterprises must be learning organizations engaged in generative learning.

Both strategic planning and the concept of learning organizations acknowledge an important point about organizations: They are all unique. They possess unique assets and are confronted with unique challenges and external circumstances, which is why the ability to set goals and plan for the future, as well as to generate original plans and solutions, are so crucial for innovation and development. Since each is different, what works for one may not work for others and an organization must have a clear understanding of its own strengths, goals, and values in order to make an informed decision about what course of action will be most effective in its particular circumstances. To make all of this more complicated, all of these unique factors interact and influence one another in specific ways, meaning that to understand an organization's true circumstances, it is necessary to not only look at the base conditions present but also the ways in which these combine and affect one another.

Systems theory is one structure of thinking that has attempted to provide a means for addressing business and organizational complexity. It conceives of groupings of things, such as organizations, as systems and attempts to analyze how elements within the system interact with each other as well as with elements outside the system. It can be visualized as a tinker toy in which the nodes represent variable characteristics and connecting rods represent the relationship between variables. This way of thinking gives a greater sense of the complexity of things. Any impact on the system spreads throughout the system based on the pattern of connections and on the nature of the relationships between connected elements. The visual model points out the probability of feedback loops and unintended consequences. Simplistic approaches to growth often get caught in cycles of unintended consequences as competitors and other external forces respond to changes in the environment.

Systems theory categorizes systems as closed or open, meaning how readily external elements can enter or impact the system and vice versa. It also looks at the exchange of energy (which could include information) between elements in the system as well as between the system and the outside and the effects this has on the functioning of the system. It is important to note that, while systems theory acknowledges that material entering the system from outside has the potential to cause disruptions, a heavily closed system is not the solution as it is likely to use up all its internal energy or resources and break down. Rather, systems need to have the ability to absorb, accommodate, or change with these influxes (Tamas, 2000). The social enterprises described in the case studies not only must be open systems, but have the capacity to act as a gateway to positive external forces.

Complexity science is an approach to thinking that includes systems theory and the need for learning structures. As an emerging approach to research, complexity science is not a single theory, but a collection of conceptual tools from an array of disciplines (Benham-Hutchins & Clancy, 2010; Paley & Gail, 2011). Complexity science has been pursued in both natural (i.e., mathematics) and social sciences (i.e., ecology), and has become increasingly popular in the health literature (University of Victoria, 2018).

Complexity science is concerned with complex intellectual problems that are dynamic, unpredictable, and multidimensional, consisting of a collection of interconnected relationships and parts. Unlike traditional "cause and effect" or linear thinking, complexity science is characterized by nonlinearity. According to Miles (2009), complex systems and problems require more than simplistic linear thinking. With a complexity science perspective, there is an appreciation of the complex, dynamic, and interconnected relationships occurring within a complex system or problem (Fisher, 2009).

Considering the public and population health issues of obesity or chronic disease, there are a multitude of factors and relationships that contribute to the problem. Therefore, a public and population health intervention requires an approach that can account for the complexity of the issue. In other words, public health professionals can be more effective if they understand the complex relationships that are occurring, rather than reducing problems to their smaller parts (Miles, 2009).

Likewise the fast-moving business world faces an interconnected set of systems that are dynamic and unpredictable. Focusing on simply growing your business might lead to the trap of linear thinking. One might conclude that just reducing production costs and prices will cause greater sales and market share, or if one just defines better the target market and advertises more, everything will be fine. Many very large corporations like Nokia, Kodak, and General Motors have lost their footing because they focused too narrowly on just making their product better or cheaper. Some, like Fannie Mae, became so large that they could no longer turn the battleship around fast enough to respond to changing currents.

Developing the organization broadly, becoming a dynamic learning organization, more able to respond to rapid change but with the sextant focused on a clear set of guiding values, might make survival in the lightning fast world more possible. As we shall see, part of comprehensive business development might be stronger relations to the various communities within which it operates, including the entrepreneurial skills and environment of those communities.

All of the above approaches provide ways of thinking about economics in more systemic and wide-reaching ways than simply how to make the most money as quickly as possible. As such, they promote a more development-based approach that could foster stronger and more resilient businesses and, thus, lead to a more stable economy in the long run. However, this is not enough to fully address wealth inequality. As explained in the previous chapter, areas and individuals in poverty have to overcome many significant barriers before economic goals of any kind, let alone economic development, can become viable. Therefore, in addition to the businesses themselves, it is necessary to also examine the environments in which the business exists or would exist. The following section applies some of the same modes of thinking to the business of community economic development.

Community and Economic Development

So far, these conceptual models and approaches discussed have been applied to business organizations, but they are equally viable at the community level. In community economic development, we can also define the distinction between simple growth and complex development that also relates to the need for social entrepreneurship and improved wealth equality.

In order to more fully explore the role communities play in social entrepreneurship, it is first necessary to establish what a community is. A community can be defined as any group of people with a common interest. The common interest can be a physical location such as a neighborhood, a craft or guild, a hobby, a profession, or an intellectual pursuit. Community development means to guide a community toward achieving the goals that relate to its common purpose. In the various cases presented in this book, the community central to each case study has a geographic focus such as a neighborhood, city, nation, or tribal territory, but with other strong common interests as well. One of those strong interests is the development of the local economy.

Growth versus Development in Community Economic Development

Many geographic communities are focused on economic growth as an overriding imperative. This may be a natural propensity toward linear thinking. A geographic community can grow in many ways. It can increase its population, the number of new buildings, its tax base, or in economic activities. All these forms of growth are desirable in many circumstances and can bring benefits to the community and its members. However, simplistic pursuit of growth can also bring problems, as witnessed in many communities.

Rapid growth in population without concomitant expansion in infrastructure to serve the population often results in dislocations such as a shortage of parking, traffic jams, inadequate space for recreation and crime, to name a few. A more holistic, systemic approach to community development will be more sensitive to complexities that cause negative system feedback and unintended consequences.

Historically, the community economic development profession has engaged in this linear thinking, disparagingly labeled "smoke stack chasing." The philosophy has been, "Growth is good, and the way to growth is to find outside companies willing to move to the community." The argument has been that this would attract new residents from the outside, expanding the population and providing additional customers for local businesses, leading to more construction of housing and commercial facilities and additional tax base. This policy sometimes involves offering tax breaks and other incentives to outside firms as attraction strategies.

While there is nothing inherently wrong with this approach, its simplistic application without thought for the complex social and economic structure of the community might produce unintended consequences. For one thing, there are very few "smoke stacks" to chase in a mature economy. The number of new factories built each year (about 8,000 to 10,000) (U.S. Bureau of Labor Statistics, 2018) is about 1/10 the number of municipalities in the United States (approximately 90,000) (Quora.com 2018). It seems nearly every community has an industrial park with many empty lots. Moreover, a high percentage of the new industrial facilities are small local operations. The number of major industrial facilities employing more than 1,000 people is very small, much smaller than the 10,000 per year figure. In fact, in 2007 there was only a total of about 1,000 such plants and the number has been declining rapidly (Holmes, 2011).

Too many resources directed at a pure growth strategy robs the community of focus and commitment to a fuller approach to economic development. Even when a community succeeds, unexpected economic feedback loops can do damage. One small community near Detroit, for example, succeeded in attracting a new Ford Motor Company factory several decades ago. It was considered a great success story for the small city. The hourly wage level paid by Ford was much higher than for most of the small businesses in the community, and the presence of the large employer caused all wages in the community to increase. While good in some ways, this higher cost of employment caused many of the previously existing small business to go out of business. A few years later, the plant cut back employment significantly from what was originally promised. But, wage-level expectations remained high. Ultimately, this left the community with less large factory employment and fewer successful small businesses (Saline, Michigan, source: the city manager). This is a small example of a common story.

Outsider-driven growth can not be achieved in a way that violates the values of the community. Does a large firm facing stringent price competition in the world market respond well to local environmental concerns? Are local efforts to preserve historic buildings respected? Is the diversity of the local population enhanced or reduced by the influx of outsiders? Will fair-wage and fair-trade traditions be maintained? Will the outside corporation have any incentive to promote local entrepreneurship? Even if the large outside firm were socially responsible, would they have enough understanding of the local community to do the right thing, or would they be a bull in a china shop?

Thus, true development of a community requires careful locally driven planning to ensure it is both achievable and amenable to the community. Further, the long-term achievement of both growth and development goals likely requires achieving some intermediate objectives or strengthening of the foundations of the community. Foundational concerns might include safety and security; respect for the variety and diversity of people who live and work in, and visit, the community; maintaining the physical infrastructure; and promoting the businesses that support and serve the community.

Outsider-driven growth, taken to the extreme, across many states and communities might also lead to greater wealth inequality as the firms attracted in such a way are owned by outsiders and distribute profits to outside shareholders. Greater emphasis on building on local skills and abilities, developing the local entrepreneurial capacity and culture, and promoting local successes might lead to a broader base of wealth growth and sharing. It might also lead to a greater long-term commitment to the community including a greater understanding of the complexity of the local community.

The Community Development Society understands the need to build a strong and complex community foundation. Their stated principles of good community development are as follows:

– Promote active and *representative participation* toward enabling all community members to meaningfully influence the decisions that affect their lives.
– Engage community members in *learning* about and understanding community issues, and the economic, social, environmental, political, psychological, and other impacts associated with alternative courses of action.
– *Incorporate the diverse interests* and cultures of the community in the community development process; and disengage from support of any effort that is likely to adversely affect the disadvantaged members of a community.
– Work actively to enhance the *leadership capacity* of community members, leaders, and groups within the community.
– Be open to using the full range of *action strategies* to work toward the long-term sustainability and well-being of the community (Community Development Society, 2018).

Asset-Oriented Community Development

It is important for any community to understand what it has that is already valuable. This idea of looking at the strengths in a community rather than the deficits is one of the main features of Asset-Based Community Development (ABCD) (Kretzmann & McKnight, 1993). ABCD can be defined as "an approach that catalyzes change and development based on utilizing the existing gifts and capacities of people and their communities."

The principles of ABCD are:

1. Focus on the positive aspects of the community. While needs-based community development emphasizes the problems or deficits of a community and how to solve them, ABCD attempts to focus on what is already strong in the community and works to hone and leverage existing strengths.
2. Everyone in the community has gifts. Each person in a community has something to contribute.
3. Relationship building is important. People must be connected for sustainable community development to take place.
4. Citizens are the center. Citizens should be viewed as the principle actors in community development not simply as recipients of services or outside expertise.
5. Leadership means involving others. Leaders should not command or be viewed as above others, but should work to involve a broad base of community members in every action.
6. Do not assume the public is apathetic. Listen to what people are interested in.
7. Community decisions should come from conversations where people are heard. Technocrats should not make decisions in isolation, based solely on data.
8. Ask. Asking for ideas is more sustainable than giving solutions.
9. Create an inside-out organization. Citizens and local community members are in control.
10. Institutions exist to serve the community not direct it. Outside institutions should create opportunities then step back (Kretzmann & McKnight, 1993).

Some of the tools of ABCD are:

1. Capacity inventory. An inventory of local capacities that are to be respected, honed, and utilized including:
    a. Personal skills: Examples of these skills can include computer and internet knowledge, listening, wallpapering, carpentry, sewing, and babysitting.
    b. Community skills.
    c. Enterprise interests and experiences. This includes experience in business and personal ideas for starting a business.
2. Asset mapping. One of the tools of ABCD frequently involves the use of asset maps to keep track of the various resources and skills present in the community and how these relate to and can enhance one another.
3. Time banks. Time banks encourage people to use their capacities to help one another, thus connecting people in new ways.

This use of asset mapping and time banks puts the focus back on the unique qualities of individual communities as they emphasize that there is not one prescripted skill set that must be present in a community. Instead, they aim to promote awareness and productive use of each community's individual skill set. They also provide tools to help community members more easily access needed resources in accordance with the idea that ABCD focuses on empowering community members to make improvements themselves, rather than relying on outside assistance. It puts faith in informal organizations of ordinary people rather than professional institutions staffed by "outside experts." This model has many useful insights considering the business and community theories explored above.

For one thing, professional organizations, which may work in several communities and, at the least, are organized outside the community, may not be keyed into the unique characteristics of the particular community. In addition, such organizations may have standardized ways of doing things based on "expert" conventional wisdom of how such situations should be handled. In governmental bureaucracies, these conventions may be codified in administrative law. This makes generative learning more difficult and simplifies the individual complexity presented in community systems. Further, putting decisions regarding a community in the hands of outsiders reduces the "on the ground" knowledge that can be brought to bear in situations like strategic planning. When determining goals and how best to achieve them, it stands to reason that community members themselves would have the best understanding of what their goals are and how they can most effectively achieve them; and therefore, making them central in the planning process is key to its success. Local citizens understand the complex social and economic structure of their community.

Further, ABCD argues that all individuals have "gifts," assets, or skills that can be brought to bear in a beneficial way. It is important to recognize that communities also have assets that can be leveraged for development. Sometimes these assets are an amalgamation of the individual assets of community members. For example, an important asset of a community might be the businesses that are located there. Businesses provide essential services, and employment. They sometimes offer meeting places for local residents that allow for both spontaneous and planned interaction and occasionally offer tangential services, as will be shown in the Irish pub example in a later chapter. A community's strongest asset might be the special skills and abilities of its residents, everything from computer programming to carpentry. A community's strengths might be embedded in the institutions that are located there or that serve the community including educational and religious institutions, hospitals, and nonprofit organizations. Many of these institutions promote or spin off other institutions that serve the community in special ways. Religious organizations often create housing subsidiaries for senior or moderate-income housing. Universities sponsor special charter schools. Local police organize basketball camps. However, a community can also have unique assets that are not based on an amalgamation of individual assets. Such valuable assets might include physical assets such as the forest that will be discussed in one case study in a later chapter. A community's assets might be a beautiful landscape that attracts residents and visitors. It might be a special history or historical artifact. These are only a few examples of the myriad assets that have been leveraged by various communities for development purposes.

Another significant aspect of ABCD is its emphasis on relationships—between individuals or between organizations composed of individuals, which bear a close resemblance to what is formally known as social capital. The foundational objectives of a community might require building a stronger network of interactions between community members and increasing social capital (Mathie, 2015). This can be seen in the discussion in the preceding chapter of this book about how poverty can cause breakdowns of trust between community members or between a community and the outside world, with significant repercussions.

Systems theory refers to this as being "internally closed," meaning the parts of the system that is the community are isolated from each other and, as system theory points out, being overly closed has a negative impact because it prevents the exchange of resources. Fostering a more open system promotes the exchange of energy—according to ABCD through the exercise of the abilities or "gifts" of individuals—which can lead the system to become stronger overall. Extensive connections between individuals are required for a community to become a learning organization in which individuals share knowledge and teach one another, making them more able to respond to rapid outside changes affecting the community.

This leverage of social capital is crucial in terms of community strategic planning as well, particularly regarding the aspect of stakeholder participation. At every stage in the process, strategic planning argues the importance of assessing the needs of stakeholders and deciding how best to serve those needs as part of the planning process. Sometimes stakeholder participation is indirect with the planning committee simply asking stakeholders what they want and then coming up with the "best method" of achieving this based on their own expertise, a method which may or may not be achievable or desirable for the stakeholders themselves. However, many strategic planning organizations are starting to operate more in line with ABCD principles by moving toward more direct participation of stakeholders not only in the setting of goals but also in decisions about the best methods of achieving those goals.

It is worth noting that, depending on the specific political, cultural, or physical conditions affecting a community, it may opt to create one large enterprise in which the majority of community members participate and have a say in the governance of, as is the case with the Ixtlan forestry group and the Alaskan native corporations explored in Chapters 9 and 10 of this book. It is important to keep in mind that while such organizations function slightly differently and may simplify some aspects of community development, they are still built on the unique gifts of members and need to be cognizant of addressing the needs of stakeholders, just like a community that contains many separate, smaller enterprises.

Clearly, ABCD provides some valuable tools to promote community growth and, especially, complex, foundational development. However, it may not provide a comprehensive picture of the situation. As explained in the last chapter, the problems associated with wealth inequality are real and systemic and addressing them may require more resources than any one community initially possesses. Certainly, focusing on the strengths of a community and giving all stakeholders a voice are valuable approaches that can provide much benefit. Yet, naming and studying the challenges facing a given community can provide more detailed information on how to address them, using those community strengths. Likewise, especially in communities struggling with poverty, it is likely that certain information or resources necessary for improvement may not initially be present and an initial influx of these may be needed to get the development projects off the ground. Certainly, communities should be empowered to utilize these resources in their own best interest, but it is also important to be wary of viewing communities as too much of a closed system. As stated in systems theory, the healthy exchange between a community and external entities is an important factor in the development of the system. The key here is to have a balance between strengthening the community internally and acknowledging what is needed from outside ... and obtaining those things in a productive way. In fact, the tendency toward closed systems and the drawbacks thereof can be seen in all levels of society from the isolation of neighbors in urban areas, to the ghettoization of areas in poverty, all the way up to isolationist policies on the national level Considering that the single issue of closed versus open has such wide ranging impact on so many levels it is no surprise that, overall, many of the same issues concerning growth versus development that apply to businesses can also be applied to communities. In addition, there is a vital symbiotic relationship between communities and the businesses located within them, and it is this relationship that social entrepreneurship explores and seeks to enhance.

Simplistic approaches to community economic growth are an almost natural outcome of linear thinking about the functioning of the local community and economy and the urge to produce growth. Yet, a lack of understanding about the complexity of the local economic system can expose the community to many perils. Complexity theory, including systems analysis can provide warnings about the possible unintended consequences of outsider-drive economic development policies. Starting with an asset-oriented approach to community development helps learning communities to focus on the talents and resources that already exist and to develop them in a broad-based way. But a community should not attempt to be too much of a closed system. Outside forces will always be influencing the internal system in both good and bad ways. The community economic development strategy must take into account these forces and engage not just in adaptive thinking that responds to what has happened in the past, but generative thinking that looks to innovative responses. Social entrepreneurship is one component of that response that can lead to a broader and more foundational creation of wealth in the community and society as a whole.

The Link to Social Entrepreneurship and Innovation

It should be clear that the authors are advocating a development-oriented approach to economic development because it creates an environment that supports the development of entrepreneurs, and a "big tent" approach to doing so. The more the individuals who have access to this support, the more widely the opportunity to generate individual, family and community wealth is spread. Social entrepreneurs engaged in social innovation that focuses on supporting commercial entrepreneurship are the catalysts. Social entrepreneurs do not create economic wealth and, therefore, can not directly affect wealth inequality. They can create other kinds of wealth (community wealth, if you will), however, that makes economic wealth building that is good for the community possible.

This is where the concept of social entrepreneurship comes in, as it provides a potential system for striking this balance between internal and external, business and community. On a basic level, innovation is a component of development rather than growth, as a new idea may take time and resources to generate and make viable. Then it will require more time and resources to implement, especially as this may require changes from how things were done in the past, all before it produces any kind of material returns. Thus innovation requires a commitment to doing something new, that may be beneficial in the long run, rather than simply trying to do the same thing more. Entrepreneurship being a form of innovation, an environment supportive of development will be more likely to allow entrepreneurship to flourish. Thus, development on the community level can make conditions more conducive to local entrepreneurship and the positive changes it can bring. The basic premise at work here is that individual success will benefit the community as a whole, through such things as job creation, influx of wealth, and inspirational models.

Entrepreneurship also ties back to the premise in ABCD of bringing individual skills to bear, as its innovative nature allows for designing a system that will most fully utilize the unique strengths of those involved. However, based on the understanding that entrepreneurs are made and not born, it is logical to assume that certain communities, especially overly closed ones may lack the resources to "make" entrepreneurs at least at first. As expressed in the conceptual model underlying the RISE training system discussed in Chapter 4, the skills of running a business, of assessing the market and determining need, are learnable (Lyons & Lyons, 2015) and, even if some individuals in the community would possess the ability to deduce these skills on their own, receiving formal training from an outside organization could certainly streamline the process and allow their innovation to reach the point of providing benefit to themselves and the community more quickly.

Starting a business or even researching an innovation requires access to resources and an initial influx of capital, as well as a ready market for the innovation, none of which may be present inside the community, at least in enough quantity and, especially in more closed communities, individuals may lack the knowledge or ability to seek them outside the community on their own. Or, they may exist in the community, but the entrepreneur is unaware of them, can not afford them, or faces a transaction barrier to acquiring them. Existing businesses, be they branches of external corporations or local businesses, should see it in their own enlightened self interest to develop the community by setting up systems to provide the resources to promote entrepreneurship in the community.

Social enterprises can provide start-up capital as well as networking development to connect entrepreneurs to investors, resource vendors and those who can market or distribute the finished product. Finally, lack of successful role models in the community can impede the development of entrepreneurial skills or even the consideration of entrepreneurship as a viable path. However, many social enterprise organizations include mentorship programs that involve matching new entrepreneurs to those with more experience who can provide inspiration as well as practical assistance.

None of the above is meant to undercut the validity of the basic premise of ABCD: the primacy of the self-directed use of individual gifts. Rather, social enterprise provides tools to help those gifts be used to the fullest extent possible. Further, as the new enterprises benefit the community and it becomes more successful and prosperous, more of these tools, such as financial capitol and role models, will be available within the community itself. Even then, an overly closed system is not ideal. Yet, as enterprises in the community develop, the ability to network and access resources outside the community can become part of the community skill set, a gift that those in the know can provide to others to further aid community development. This concept is elaborated by Granovetter's concept of blending "agency," the work of the individual, and "context," the environment (Granovetter, 2017).

Through these means, social enterprise can create a virtuous cycle of community development and stakeholder participation with a move toward greater self-sufficiency, or even exchange with other communities through entrepreneurial ecosystems. Actually, entrepreneurial ecosystems are focused on exchanges within the community/region. Through identifying entrepreneurs and sources of their support, they attempt to build the networks of social capital that help the flow of resources to the entrepreneurs that need them. However, it is important to keep in mind that the need to set goals and evaluate needs as well the potential benefit of outside training and assistance do not end with the initial phase of getting the community's enterprise(s) up and running. As system theory explains, systems evolve and any change of energy in the system or in the exchange of energy with the world outside will cause the system itself to change to adapt to the shifting energy. Thus, as a community grows and develops it will change, which may require its approaches to various matters to be revised. This is why reassessment and evaluation are important steps in the strategic planning process, to ensure that the initial approach works in the system's current form and that the needs of stakeholders are still being served. Thus, it is crucial to maintain this process to address the unique challenges communities and enterprises will face as they change and evolve, even in a positive direction.

Specifically, success in community and economic development can bring difficult consequences for members of a community. Gentrification is one example. If a struggling neighborhood is successful at improving the economic and physical situation of the neighborhood, rents might go up, forcing out long-time renter residents. Many of the people owning homes might be elderly people who have lived there for a long time. Increases in property values might make taxes too high for them to continue to pay. If a simplistic solution focused narrowly on economic growth is applied, as opposed to a broader type of economic development, problems related to gentrification might be more likely. Also, if one of the businesses in the community is highly successful, it might need to expand or might require more parking causing other buildings to be torn down. This could be a disadvantage to other businesses or adjacent residents. A successful company might generate greater truck traffic that could disturb residential areas, adding noise or dust or causing people to feel less safe.

On the other side of the equation, if a local business is highly successful one must fear that it will move out, causing job loss and loss of value to the local community. This might happen if expansion needs can not be accommodated or if an outside company purchases the local business. Local businesses that do not feel appreciated by the local community, or do not feel integrated into the community such that they feel no ownership in the community's wellbeing, are more likely to move out. Even if the business stays, initial success might cause the business to become more institutionalized and internationally competitive, meaning that it loses track of its initial values that tied it to the community. To compete, it might feel it must cut out anything that draws resources away from immediate competitive success.

For a community to respond, survive, and thrive in a rapidly changing world, it must do more than pursue simplistic growth strategies. It must respect the complexity of the community, seek out the strengths and skills of its individual citizens, identify, utilize, and develop its internal assets, work to generate its own resources, and plan together as a learning community. As discussed throughout this book, entrepreneurship is not just about creating high-tech businesses. It is about building broad-based wealth by encouraging a wide-variety of small businesses utilizing the myriad talents found in many parts of the community and guiding these entrepreneurs toward the knowledge, skills, and emotional support needed to succeed and ultimately give back to their community.

An important part of this economic development strategy is the assessment, encouragement, and development of the entrepreneurial talents of creative members of the community. The following chapters will describe the concept of social entrepreneurship in detail and provide in-depth, multifaceted, case-study examples of the successes and challenges of this approach to addressing wealth inequality.

References

Blackerby, P. (2003). History of strategic planning. Retrieved from http://www.blackerbyassoc. com/history.html. Accessed July 31, 2018. This document was originally published in *Armed Forces Comptroller* 39 (1) (Winter 1994): 23–24. This document has been slightly revised, primarily by adding the Table of Contents.

Benham-Hutchins, M., & Clancy, T. (2010). Social networks as embedded complex adaptive systems. *JONA* 40(9): 352–356.

Community Development Society. (2018). Principles of good practice. Retrieved from https://www.comm-dev.org/about/principles-of-good-practice. Accessed January 10, 2018.

Fisher, L. (2009). *The perfect swarm: The science of complexity in everyday life.* New York: Basic Books, 260 pp.

Gephart, M., Marsick, J., Van Buren, M., Spiro, M., & Senge, P. (1996). Learning organizations come alive. *Training and Development* 50 (12): 34–45.

Granovetter, M. (2017). *Society and economy: Framework and principles.* Cambridge, MA: The Belknap Press of Harvard University Press.

Hamlin R.E. ,Vanravensway, J., Mastej, M., & Hamlin. A. (forthcoming). Strategic planning in U.S. municipalities. In Hintea, C., Profiroiu, M., Ticlau, & T.C., *Strategic Planning in Local Communities: A Cross-National Study in 8 Countries.* Palgrave.

Hintea, C, Hudrea, A., & Hamlin, R.E. (2003). *Strategic planning in public administration*. Bucherest, Romania: Tritonic Books. 2013. 115 pp. ISBN 978-606-93440-1-9. (65.012.4) Funded by a grant from the European Union.

Holmes, T.J. (2011). The case of the disappearing large-employer manufacturing plant: Not much of a mystery after all. Economic Policy Papers of the Federal Reserve of Minneapolis. 18 pp.

Kretzmann, J., & McKnight, J. (1993). *Building communities from the inside out: Toward finding and mobilizing a community's assets*. Evanston, IL: Institute for Policy Research.

Lyons, T.S., & Lyons, J.S. (2015). *A skills assessment approach to operationalizing entrepreneur skills theory*. White paper. Morristown, NJ: Lyons Entrepreneurial Assessment Partners, LLC.

Mathie, A., & Cunningham G. (2003). From clients to citizens: Asset-based Community Development as a strategy for community-driven development, Development in Practice, 13:5,474–486, DOI: 10.1080/0961452032000125857

McGill, M., Slocum, J., & Lei, D. (1992). Management practices in learning organizations. *Organizational Dynamics* 21 (1): 5–17.

Miles, A. (2009). Complexity in medicine and healthcare: People and systems, theory and practice. *Journal of Evaluation in Clinical Practice* 15, 409–410.

Onelook Thesaurus. Retrieved from http://onelook.com/thesaurus/. Accessed August 5, 2018.

Paley, J., & Gail, E. (2011). Complexity theory as an approach to explanation in healthcare: A critical discussion. *International Journal of Nursing Studies* 48: 269–279.

Quora.com Retrieved from https://www.quora.com/How-many-towns-counties-and-cities-are-in-the-USA. Accessed July 10, 2018.

Senge, P. (1990). *The fifth discipline: The art and practice of the learning organization*. New York: Double Day/Currency. 424 pp.

Tamas, A., Whitehorse, Y., & Ontario, A. (2000). Systems theory in community development. Symanticscholar.org 8 pp.

United State Department of Labor, Bureau of Labor Statistics, Industries at a glance, Manufacturing NAICS 33–33. Retrieved from https://www.bls.gov/iag/tgs/iag31-33.htm. Accessed July 22, 2018.

Vanravensway, J., & Hamlin, R.E. (2015). Strategic planning in U.S. municipalities. Transylvanian Review of Administrative Sciences. Special Issue. Pp. 55–70.

University of Victoria. (2018). Complexity science in brief. Retrieved from https://www.uvic.ca/research/ groups/cphfri/assets/docs/Complexity_Science_in_Brief.pdf. Accessed July 20, 2018.

Chapter 3
The Rise of Entrepreneurship as an Economic Development Strategy

A survey by the National Association of State Development Agencies (NASDA) in the United States in 1998 found that of the approximately $2 billion in total annual investment in economic development by state governments, less than 1 percent went to the development of entrepreneurship (NASDA, 1998). In an article in the 2006 edition of *The Municipal Year Book*, Lyons and Koven (2006) reported on the results of a 2004 survey by the International City/County Management Association (ICMA) of chief administrative officers in cities with a population over 10,000 and counties over 50,000. When it came to economic development strategies, 44 percent of respondents indicated that a focus of their efforts was business attraction, 41 percent listed business retention, while only 19 percent listed business development (entrepreneurship) as a focus (p. 14). This low status of entrepreneurship support in the state and local economic development tool kit was symptomatic of the field until recently.

There are two primary reasons for this. First, for decades the predominant theory as to why entrepreneurs were successful was the so-called traits theory. This view held that entrepreneurs were born into their roles, possessing innate traits or characteristics that made them who they were (Greenberg & Sexton, 1988; Huefner & Hunt, 1994; Schumpeter, 1991). The message to economic developers was that there is no need to try to develop entrepreneurs. All that can be done is to attempt to "pick winners" (find those that have the requisite traits) and assist them (Lichtenstein et al., 2004; Lichtenstein & Lyons, 2010). Second, entrepreneurship support is a form of "patient" economic development. That is, it takes a long-term commitment of time and resources to develop entrepreneurs and their enterprises (Markley et al., 2015; Lyons & Koven, 2006) and the results are slow to materialize and geographically fragmented in their impact. As a result, this strategy is less attractive to politicians and the economic developers who work for them, as the outcomes are more incremental and less immediate than are those of business attraction and retention.

Over the years, traits theory was tested by research and remains unproven. Researchers have been unable to find even one unique innate trait that is applicable to all entrepreneurs. Attention has shifted to other explanations for entrepreneurship success, including behavior, cognition, and skills, which are developable (Carter et al., 1996; Shane & Venkataraman, 2000; Minniti & Bygrave, 2001; Lichtenstein & Lyons, 2001; Lyons et al., 2007). Recent research supports

DOI 10.1515/9781547400461-003

the role of entrepreneurship in significantly generating new economic development (Eliasson & Henrekson, 2004; Kane, 2010; Reedy & Litan, 2011; Hafer, 2013). This shift in thinking and focus has resulted in economic development efforts that now include, and are sometimes driven by, the creation of entrepreneurship support systems locally and regionally. "Entrepreneurial ecosystems" or "entrepreneurial communities" are the names used to denote these new systems.

In this chapter we examine the major strategies available to economic developers and place entrepreneurship support among them. We then look at how entrepreneurial activity has in the past, and continues to, benefit the economies in which it takes place. We conclude by discussing the new forms entrepreneurship-focused economic development has been taking, as this type of economic development rises to prominence.

The Three Major Economic Development Strategies

Economic development has become a complex field over the years. It is characterized in many ways, but the simplest way to depict it is as a three-legged stool, with each leg representing one of the core economic development strategies—business attraction, business retention, and business creation. To put this in other words, the economic developer seeks to lure businesses from outside the community or region to that locale, to keep the businesses currently located there from moving elsewhere, or to encourage the formation and growth of new businesses in the place in question. Typically, economic development organizations (EDOs) attempt to do all three; however, they may emphasize one over the others.

To enable a better understanding of these strategic choices, we examine each in more detail. The tactics by which these strategies are most often pursued, and the strengths and limitations of each approach, are discussed.

Business Attraction

The chief assumptions underlying the pursuit of a business attraction strategy are:
- That the business being pursued can be incentivized to either leave its current location or to establish a branch in the jurisdiction trying to attract it.
- If that business is successfully attracted, it will generate jobs, tax base, and other economic benefits to the community commensurate with the investment made.
- That the business will live up to the promises it makes to the community in exchange for the incentives it receives.

Most EDOs that pursue an attraction strategy use financial and/or non-financial incentives as tools for marketing their jurisdiction to outside companies or as bargaining chips in negotiations with companies that have already preliminarily identified the community as a desirable location (Koven & Lyons, 2010). Financial incentives might include grants, loans, tax-exempt bonds, tax abatements, tax exemptions, among others (Koven & Lyons, 2010). Non-financial incentives may include site development, industrial/office parks, enterprise/smart zones, and customized training (Koven & Lyons, 2010). Increasingly, the quality of the workforce is an important incentive to business attraction. Companies are looking for human resources that have the education and training necessary to make them job ready. This has become so important that some EDOs have made talent attraction part of their business attraction strategy. As an example, the Regional Economic Development Corporation (REDI) of Idaho has been involved in strengthening STEM education, creating a program for talent attraction, and building a business internship program, among other initiatives, in their region in the eastern part of that state (Allen, 2016).

Being able to find an appropriate labor force at all job levels has become a growing problem. In the United States, this is widely attributed to six factors (DePillis, 2018; Dorfman, 2017; Megan, 2017; Ydstie, 2017). For higher-paying jobs, these are (1) a lack of appropriate education and training for the work available, (2) unrealistic expectations of employers, and (3) a geographic mismatch between talent and jobs. For lower-wage jobs, the factors are (1) low wages; (2) the lack of a clear immigration policy, which restricts the flow of immigrant labor; and (3) more workers being unable to fill or keep jobs, due to increased drug addiction, particularly the opioid epidemic. Many of these factors have their roots in wealth inequality and/or serve to exacerbate it.

The community's quality of life is still another incentive used in business attraction. Features such as recreational assets, scenic beauty, a strong arts and culture scene, fine dining, good schools, and so forth are commonly cited as being attractive to white collar employers, such as corporate headquarters (Koven & Lyons, 2010). The link is often made between quality of life and quality of the local workforce. Richard Florida (2002) has long argued that a strong quality of life attracts the "creative class," which, in turn, makes a place attractive to businesses.

There is not universal agreement on the benefits of the business attraction strategy. Supporters argue that incentives to attract businesses yield returns on investment that are worth the risk, that new businesses in the community generate tax revenues that are vital to providing public services, and that businesses are important community members that deserve the community's support (Koven & Lyons, 2010). A study in Virginia found that manufacturing jobs created by business attraction efforts could reduce income inequality. It should be clarified that this was found to be true for only manufacturing and not the professional and business services sectors, which tended to increase income inequality (Shuai, 2015).

Opponents of business attraction argue that it often creates unproductive competition among EDOs; that benefiting companies does not ensure their loyalty to the community; that extending incentives to businesses will only beget more demands for incentives; that companies often are not held accountable for their end of the attraction bargain; and that dollars spent on attraction could be better spent on health, education and social challenges (Koven & Lyons, 2010; Helbig, 2017). In fairness, EDOs have recently improved their efforts to hold businesses receiving incentives accountable, including the institution of so-called claw-back clauses in contracts that allow the community to "demand a refund" when businesses do not fulfill their promises.

The results of the Virginia study, noted above, regarding the relationship between business attraction and income inequality are not surprising. Attracting manufacturing jobs, which was found to reduce income inequality, tends to benefit lower income individuals by providing well-paying jobs that require less education. Attracting professional jobs, which was found to increase income inequality, benefits individuals who are already typically better educated and earning higher incomes. It should be noted, however, that income equality does not ensure wealth equality, which is the subject of this book. As Oliver and Shapiro (2006) point out, the income gap has been shrinking, but the wealth gap continues to increase.

Perhaps the strongest criticism of the business attraction strategy is that because there are fewer businesses to recruit and there is greater competition for attracting these companies, such programs have become defensive (a jurisdiction cannot afford *not* to have one) and very expensive. Relatively speaking, business retention creates more jobs than does attraction and requires a lower public investment (Helbig, 2017). This leads us to a discussion of the business retention strategy.

Business Retention

While business attraction has long been the most popular strategy among EDOs, it is widely acknowledged by economic developers that 75 percent of job growth comes from businesses that are already located in the given community (Rausch, 2006: 1). This means that retaining these businesses should be a very high priority.

When pursuing a business retention strategy, EDOs are not only seeking to keep resident companies in their communities but to encourage them to grow as well. In fact, this set of activities is now more commonly referred to as business retention and expansion (BR&E).

BR&E assumes that businesses can be incentivized to remain in place and expand their capital and labor investments. The financial and non-financial incentives used by EDOs to influence this behavior on the part of businesses in their jurisdictions are essentially the same as those employed for business attraction purposes. EDOs stay in close contact with their local businesses, regularly engaging them in conversations about their needs and how well those needs are being met by the local community (Lyons & Hamlin, 2001: 37). The EDO in Allen County, OH reports that they make an average of 100 such visits every year (Rausch, 2006: 1). Lyons and Hamlin (2001) suggest two simple questions that should be regularly posed to local companies: "What single thing would make your business more successful?" and "What single action could this economic development office take that would make your business more successful?" The answers to these questions become tactics built into the EDO's BR&E strategy.

Sometimes, businesses are not entirely aware of what they need. They may realize that things are not going well but are not sure why. At this point, the business is in peril, and could be lost to the local community. BR&E becomes about retention, exclusively. A private sector consultant in Kentwood, MI, a suburb of Grand Rapids, recognized this and created the Business Reinvention Exchange. The Exchange is a no-cost monthly event that helps struggling businesses in the community to reinvent themselves by examining their current situation and using that knowledge as a springboard to setting measurable goals for their future (Daly, 2008). While these events clearly benefit the consultant's business, they also benefit the community by helping businesses in crisis to become strategic and pull themselves out of their difficulties.

In some cases, the struggles of businesses already operating in our communities stem from the status of their owner-operators and the unique challenges these pose (Durr et al., 2000). This is particularly true for smaller immigrant-owned companies. In Washington State, the Economic Development Association of Skagit County (EDASC) recognized this and, as a result, created the Latino Business Retention and Expansion Program (LBRE). LBRE seeks to address issues facing Latino business owners such as a lack of access to information, assistance, and training geared to their level of confidence in using English as a first language; a lack of business role models; and a lack of some of the skills of business (Morelli-Klima, 2013). Helping Latino business owners with these issues has resulted in some impressive impact metrics for LBRE. As an example, between its inception in 2004 and 2013, this EDO helped its client businesses to obtain nearly $3 million in loans (Morelli-Klima, 2013: 30). LBRE is a good example of a BR&E

program that focuses on needs of entrepreneurs who operate local businesses to build healthier businesses with strong ties to the community.

BR&E programs have some strong potential benefits (University of Minnesota Extension, 2017):
–   They are relatively low risk to the community that uses them.
–   They are an effective way to demonstrate to local businesses that the community cares about them.
–   They facilitate network building among various players in the community.
–   They focus on keeping what the community has, as opposed to chasing what it does not have.

On the downside, retention is not a particularly effective strategy for communities that have very little left to retain. It is also a difficult strategy to execute effectively, as it requires getting past the feelings of skepticism and mistrust that often exist between businesses and government (Lyons & Hamlin, 2001).

Business Creation

While many communities continue to cling to business attraction and retention strategies, the profile of entrepreneurship-focused economic development has risen dramatically in the past few decades. This appears to be a global phenomenon. The Global Entrepreneurship Monitor (GEM) project has found high levels of entrepreneurship activity in developing countries in Africa and Central and South America (GEM, 2017). In the United States, this might be considered a re-emergence of entrepreneurship as an economic driver. It is well documented that entrepreneurs were the leaders of this country's economic and civic development from the colonial period through the first and second Industrial Revolutions (Gunderson, 2005; Neck et al., 2017). However, toward the middle of the twentieth century, the rise of corporations and large government entities brought about an institutionalization of the United States and a departure from the focus on entrepreneurial activity (Gunderson, 2005; Neck et al., 2017). With the globalization of the economy and its accompanying intense competition, corporations have been downsizing and substituting capital for labor. They have had to become more nimble and entrepreneurial merely to survive. "Innovation" has become the buzzword of the twenty-first century, as the economy is continuously disrupted and companies must regularly reinvent themselves.

This situation has not only made corporations more conscious of the importance of entrepreneurship/innovation but has increasingly made entrepreneurship the most viable career option for many as well. While the attention of politicians in developed countries is focused on the corporate jobs lost to the outsourcing of work to cheaper labor markets in less developed countries, the reality is that many more jobs are being lost to automation. A recent report by McKinsey & Company predicts that 73 million U.S. jobs will be lost to automation by 2030, and a PriceWaterhouseCoopers report indicates that 38 percent of U.S. jobs will disappear for the same reason in that period (Manyika et al., 2017; Berriman & Hawksworth, 2017). Combining these factors with corporate pursuit of efficiencies that maximize profits to shareholders results in a situation where working for someone else in developed countries has become increasingly more difficult, and the jobs that are available around the world are increasingly less likely to sustain a good quality of life and more likely to foster wealth inequality.

Well-paying manufacturing jobs have become a thing of the past in many communities, replaced by low-paid service sector jobs. Many individuals find that they must work more than one job to generate enough revenue to support themselves and their families. They typically do not have health insurance or other benefits. While manufacturing appears to have made a bit of a comeback in some places, this is twenty-first-century manufacturing, which relies less on human labor and more on robots and other forms of automation. This situation has hit the uneducated and undereducated especially hard.

The educated are not immune to the negative impacts of the changing economy, however. The costs of a college education have soared, and many college graduates complete their degrees having amassed a sizeable debt. They enter a job market that is not well matched to their skill set or that pays too little to allow them to pay down this debt and build the assets needed to create wealth (e.g., buy a house, invest in a financial portfolio, etc.). Because many of the available jobs are located in high-cost urban areas, this group must over-pay for the essentials of living. Even when they do find jobs, they are often underpaid and receive meager, if any, benefits.

All these circumstances have made entrepreneurship the most viable alternative to traditional employment. For some, this is what the GEM project calls "necessity entrepreneurship"—starting and running a business because there are no other economic alternatives. For others, they see an opportunity to add value to the lives of a market of people, and they create a business to pursue this opportunity. GEM calls this group "opportunity entrepreneurs."

EDOs have sought to facilitate this entrepreneurial activity in a variety of ways. Financing tools for encouraging enterprise development have included micro-lending programs, more traditional loan programs, gap financing, and angel and venture capital (Koven & Lyons, 2010). Non-financial tools have included one-stop assistance, market identification and marketing assistance, entrepreneur mentoring and coaching, and business incubation, among others (Koven & Lyons, 2010). While these various tools and tactics have enjoyed some success, they remain fragmented and categorical in approach, thereby limiting their ability to transform an economy (Lichtenstein et al., 2004).

Despite its increasing acceptance as an economic development strategy, traditional business creation has its shortcomings. It takes time for outcomes to materialize, causing politicians and practitioners to lose patience. Its impacts are often spread widely across geographical areas, making them seem small and inconsequential relative to those of a large manufacturing facility, with its hundreds of jobs located in one place, for example. Its focus is typically on self-employment and not true entrepreneurship, which often results in very small businesses that have no capacity to grow. These small companies may provide income substitution, but they rarely foster wealth creation. However, traditional business creation is rapidly evolving into something much more systemic, which addresses these shortcomings and makes it still more attractive to economic developers. This phenomenon is discussed in greater detail in the last section of this chapter.

The Benefits of Entrepreneurship to Economies

There would seem to be a very strong consensus that entrepreneurship can be highly beneficial to local, regional, and national economies. This has long been suspected, but recent empirical research tends to lend credence to this view (van Praag & Versloot, 2007).

There is broad agreement that entrepreneurship activity creates jobs (van Praag & Versloot, 2007; Kritikos, 2014; Kauffman Foundation, 2016). High growth entrepreneurial ventures are thought to create up to 50 percent of all new jobs (Kauffman Foundation, 2016). This same study found that in a five-year period these growth ventures grew, on average, from 5.8 to 9.2 employees. Further, these entrepreneurial companies have been found to stimulate employment growth among other businesses in their region (van Praag & Versloot, 2007; Kauffman Foundation, 2016). Kritikos (2014) cautions, however, that job growth from entrepreneurship may not be immediate, and, in fact, there may be short-term job loss that results from the disruption of an economy brought on by innovation. This latter observation provides another explanation for the reluctance of politicians and EDOs to embrace entrepreneurship fully. Not only is it uncomfortable to experience a period of job loss, but also existing companies will perceive it as being in their best interest to block entrepreneurship and its resulting innovation by lobbying hard against supporting it.

Job creation is not the only economic benefit of entrepreneurial activity. Research has repeatedly shown that it fosters creativity and innovation. New products and services are created and commercialized (van Praag & Versloot, 2007). While entrepreneurs may not always be the inventors, they are the ones who assemble the resources and manage the risks required to get these products and services to the markets that need them.

One popular myth that has arisen about innovation is that it is largely focused on technological products and services. While this may be considered by many to be the glamorous side of entrepreneurship and, for that reason, garners most of the media attention, it is untrue. A recent study of high-growth start-ups by the Ewing Marion Kauffman Foundation found that these entrepreneurial ventures are quite diverse, representing most industries. Furthermore, there was a decrease in high-growth entrepreneurship in the computer hardware industry in the decade leading up to this research (Kauffman Foundation, 2016).

Recent studies also demonstrate that Schumpeter's famous concept of "creative destruction" born of entrepreneurship is a fact. Schumpeter, the Austrian economist and a pioneer in the study of entrepreneurship, argued that one of the economic benefits of entrepreneurial activity is that it refreshes an economy through creativity and innovation by replacing old products and services with new ones. This also has the effect of replacing old non-innovative companies with new ones that do innovate. This can be seen in regions where entrepreneurship has fostered competition that has forced existing businesses to either become more innovative or fail. When existing companies change or fail this leads to a restructuring of the regional economy and economic progress (Kritikos, 2014). While this process may be painful for some, in the long run, it benefits consumers and the region's economy.

This benefit manifests itself in a variety of forms. Research shows that entrepreneurs are happier, and thus more productive, than traditional employees are (Frey & Benz, 2003). This has implications for entrepreneurship within existing businesses (intrapreneurship) as well. Overall, entrepreneurship has been found to have positive spillover effects for the entire region in which it exists (van Praag & Versloot, 2007).

Kritikos (2014) makes an interesting and important observation. While economic developers and researchers often attempt to use self-employment as an indicator of entrepreneurial activity in a place, self-employment and economic development are not necessarily correlated. As noted earlier in this chapter, self-employment is not essentially well correlated with entrepreneurship. Entrepreneurs seek growth, and this is how they build wealth. Wealth creation fosters economic development in the long run. As Kritikos (2014) notes, self-employment is greatest in the places that are least developed, from urban inner cities and rural small towns in the United States to entire developing countries.

The Emerging Form of Entrepreneurship Support as an Economic Development Strategy

From an economic development perspective, it appears that entrepreneurship is well worth facilitating. However, traditional business creation has its limitations, as noted, and likely will not produce the economic transformation for which communities are hoping. So, what will?

The answer to this question lies in an emerging form of entrepreneurship support that is gaining considerable traction—the "entrepreneurial community" or "entrepreneurial ecosystem." The underlying concept here is that it is possible to identify all the players in such a system and connect them productively in a web of mutual support. This requires being able to marry successfully two important perspectives: that of the entrepreneur and that of the community.

Because the desire to support entrepreneurship as an economic development strategy came from the community, this was the dominant perspective in the early days of these activities. The focus was on the supply side—what services the community could provide that would make entrepreneurship more attractive and feasible for entrepreneurs. This led to some very creative tools for fostering entrepreneurship, but the demand for these services was assumed. Entrepreneurs were seldom asked what they needed (Kayne, 2002). It was also true that economic developers believed that if they provided these services, entrepreneurs would emerge to use them, when, in fact, active entrepreneurs create the demand for support, not the other way around (Lichtenstein & Lyons, 2001).

The business perspective was no less one-sided. Entrepreneurs did not trust economic developers to understand and address their needs. From the business perspective, it is argued that programs to support entrepreneurship should be managed by entrepreneurs. As an example, in Buenos Aires, Argentina, a city-wide program operated by local government to foster technology entrepreneurship intentionally chose a former entrepreneur as its manager (Global Endeavor, 2012). Lichtenstein et al. (2004) took this a step further by asserting that the focus of any effort to support entrepreneurship should be on the entrepreneur, and not the business.

As research and practice in entrepreneurship-focused economic development grew more sophisticated, elements of both the community and business perspectives were increasingly combined. The Edward Lowe Foundation (2002) began a body of research on "entrepreneurial communities" that found that these systems had five components: (1) a supportive infrastructure that includes everything from internet access to higher education institutions to transportation facilities, (2) a community that is supportive of entrepreneurship, (3) networking among all the parties in the entrepreneurship process, (4) a government that supports business, and (5) a diversity of sources of business financing. Lichtenstein et al. (2004) extended this line of thinking by identifying five "strategies" for building an entrepreneurial community:

1. *Be systemic in approach.* This strategy brings the many pieces of enterprise development together into a cohesive whole.
2. *Customize this system.* This recognizes the place-based nature of entrepreneurship and the uniqueness of each place.
3. *Place the focus on developing entrepreneurs.* A truly entrepreneurial community goes beyond providing services and infrastructure for entrepreneurship to facilitating the individual development of the entrepreneurs that start, grow, and sustain the community's enterprises.
4. *Include a governance mechanism for the system.* Someone(s) must be responsible for the overall operation of the system. This governance model must be different from past efforts to foster entrepreneurship, including new skills, roles, and tools to implement it.
5. *The system must be a "transformation business."* It must be evaluated as to its ability to transform the community's economy through the quality and quantity of the entrepreneurs and enterprises it nurtures.

Feld (2012) discusses a simplified model for an "entrepreneurial ecosystem" called the Boulder Thesis, which holds that a successful ecosystem possesses the following characteristics: (1) inclusivity, (2) entrepreneurs in leadership roles, (3) extensive networking, and (4) a long-term commitment to the ecosystem by the players.

Perhaps the most holistic effort to meld the community and business aspects of entrepreneurial ecosystem development comes from Markley et al. (2015). These authors blend a model for building community capacity to support entrepreneurship with a model that develops entrepreneurs and their enterprises. In this way, they take us on a good path toward a systemic, systematic, and strategic approach to creating individual and community wealth through entrepreneurship. We will explore this concept in more depth in the last chapter of this book.

References

Allen, A.W. (2016). Business attraction now includes talent attraction. *The Idaho Business Review*, Boise (June 13), N/A.

Berriman, R., & Hawksworth, J. (2017). Will robots steal our jobs? The potential impact of automation on the UK and other major economies. In PriceWaterhouseCoopers, *UK Economic Outlook* (March): 30.

Carter, N.M., Gartner, W.B., & Reynold, P.D. (1996). Exploring start-up event sequences. *Journal of Business Venturing* 11: 151–166.

Daly, P. (2008). Business reinvention strategy essential in current economy. *Grand Rapids Business Journal* 26 (50): 3.

DePillis, L. (2018). The opioid crisis is draining America's workforce. CNN Money. Retrieved from money.cnn.com/2018/02/22/news/economy/workforce-opioid-crisis/index.html. Accessed May 15, 2018.

Dorfman, J. (2017). Employers cannot fill jobs and there is no easy solution. *Forbes*/Opinion/#Economy. Retrieved from https://www.forbes.com/sites/ jeffreydorfman/2017/12/27/employers-cannot-fill-jobs-and-there-is-no-easy-solution/#590787453c46. Accessed May 15, 2018.

Durr, M., Lyons, T.S., & Lichtenstein, G.A. (2000). Identifying the unique needs of urban entrepreneurs: African American skill set development. *Race & Society* 3: 75–90.

Edward Lowe Foundation. (2002). *Building entrepreneurial communities*. Cassopolis, MI: Edward Lowe Foundation.

Eliasson, G., & Henreksen, M. (2004). William J. Baumol: An entrepreneurial economist on the economics of entrepreneurship. *Small Business Economics* 23: 1–7.

Feld, B. (2012). *Startup communities: Building an entrepreneurial ecosystem in your community*. New York: Wiley.

Florida, R. (2002). *The rise of the creative class*. New York: Basic Books.

Global Endeavor. (2012). The multiplier effect: High impact entrepreneurship lessons from Buenos Aires, Istanbul, and Amman. Policy implications. Retrieved from www.canieti.org/ Libraries/Evento_Retos_sector_TI/Fernando_Fabre_Multiplier_Effect.sflb.ashx Accessed May 14, 2018.

Greenberg, D.B., & Sexton, D.L. (1988). An interactive model of new venture initiation. *Journal of Small Business Management* 26 (3): 1–7.

Gunderson, G. (2005). *An entrepreneurial history of the United States*. Washington, DC: Beard Books.

Hafer, R.W. (2013). Entrepreneurship and state economic growth. *Journal of Entrepreneurship and Public Policy* 2, 67–79.

Huefner, J.C., & Hunt, H.K. (1994). Broadening the concept of entrepreneurship: Comparing business and consumer entrepreneurs. *Entrepreneurship Theory and Practice* 18 (3): 61–75.

Kane, T. (2010). The importance of startups in job creation and job destruction. The Kauffman Foundation. Retrieved from http://www.kauffman.org/what-we-do/research/ firm-formation-and-growth-series/the-importance-of-startups-in-job-creation-and-job-destruction. Accessed December 14, 2017.

Kauffman Foundation. (2016). The economic impact of high-growth startups, *Entrepreneurship Policy Brief*, June 7.

Kayne, J. (2002). *Promoting and supporting an entrepreneurship-based economy in Maine*. Augusta, ME: Ewing Marion Kauffman Foundation and Entrepreneurial Working Group/ Maine Small Business Commission.

Koven, S.G., & Lyons, T.S. (2010). *Economic development: Strategies for state and local practice*. Washington, DC: International City/County Management Association.

Kritikos, A.S. (2014). Entrepreneurs and their impacts on jobs and economic growth, *IZA World of Labor*, 8. doi: 10.15185/izawol.8.

Lichtenstein, G.A., & Lyons, T.S. (2001). The entrepreneurial development system: Transforming business talent and community economies. *Economic Development Quarterly* 15 (1): 3–20.

Lichtenstein, G.A., & Lyons, T.S. (2010). *Investing in entrepreneurs: A strategic approach for strengthening your regional and community economy.* Santa Barbara, CA: Praeger/ABC-CLIO.

Lichtenstein, G.A., Lyons, T.S., & Kutzhanova, N. (2004). Building entrepreneurial communities: The appropriate role of enterprise development activities. *Journal of the Community Development Society* 35 (1): 5–24.

Lyons, T.S., & Hamlin, R.E. (2001). *Creating an economic development action plan.* Westport, CT: Praeger.

Lyons, T.S., & Koven, S.G. (2006). Economic development and public policy at the local government level. In International City/County Management Association. *The Municipal Yearbook 2006.* Washington, DC: International City/County Management Association.

Manyika, J., Lund, S., Chui, M., Bughin, J., Woetzel, J., Batra, P., Ko, R., & Sanghvi, S. (2017). *Jobs lost, jobs gained: Workforce transitions in a time of automation.* San Francisco, CA: McKinsey & Company.

Markley, D.M., Lyons, T.S., & Macke, D.W. (2015). Creating entrepreneurial communities: Building community capacity for ecosystem development. *Community Development* 46 (5): 580–598.

Megan, K. (2017). Worsening labor shortages demonstrate need for immigration reform. Bipartisan Policy Center (October 30). Retrieved from https://bipartisanpolicy.org/blog/worsening-labor-shortages-demonstrate-need-for-immigration-reform/. Accessed May 15, 2018.

Minniti, M, & Bygrave, W. (2001). A dynamic model of entrepreneurial learning. *Entrepreneurship Theory and Practice* 25 (3): 5–16.

Morelli-Klima, D. (2013). Mindsets that build bridges across cultures and champion Latino small businesses. *Economic Development Journal* 12 (4): 29–34.

National Association of State Development Agencies. (1998). *State economic development expenditure survey.* Washington, DC: NASDA.

Neck, H.M., Neck, C.P., & Murray, E.L. (2017). *Entrepreneurship: The practice and mindset.* Los Angeles: Sage.

Oliver, M.L., & Shapiro, T. (2006). *Black wealth, white wealth: A new perspective on racial inequality.* New York: Routledge.

Rausch, T. (2006). Keeping the doors open: Retention is the bread and butter of economic development. *McClatchy-Tribune Business News*, November 19: 1.

Reedy, E.J., & Litan, R.E. (2011). Starting smaller; staying smaller: America's slow leak in job creation. The Kauffman Foundation. Retrieved from http://www.kauffman.org/~/media/kauffman_org/research%20reports%20and%20covers/2011/07/job_leaks_starting_smaller_study.pdf. Accessed December 14, 2017.

Schumpeter, J. (1991). Comments on a plan for the study of entrepreneurship. In R. Swedberg (Ed.). *Joseph A. Schumpeter: The economics and sociology of capitalism* (pp. 406–428). Princeton, NJ: Princeton University Press.

Shane, S., & Venkataraman, S. (2000). The promise of entrepreneurship as a field of research. *Academy of Management Review* 25 (1): 217–226.

Shuai, X. (2015). Do economic development efforts benefit all? Business attraction and income inequality. *The Review of Regional Studies* 45: 35–56.

University of Minnesota Extension. (2017). Business retention & expansion (BR&E), BR&E Strategies Program: Benefits. Retrieved from https://www.extension.umn.edu/community/business-retention/strategies/benefits. Accessed December 21, 2017.

van Praag, C.M. & Versloot, P.H. (2007). What is the value of entrepreneurship? A review of recent research. *Small Business Economics* 29 (4): 351–382.

Ydstie, J. (2017). U.S. employers struggle to match workers with open jobs. NPR, *All Things Considered* (August 31). Retrieved from https://www.npr.org/2017/08/31/547646709/u-s-employers-struggle-to-match-workers-with-open-jobs. Accessed May 15, 2018.

Chapter 4
How Entrepreneurship Can Be Fostered in a Way That Mitigates Economic Inequality

Essential to making the case for entrepreneurship as an approach to mitigating wealth inequality is establishing the meaning of this term.[1] While there is not complete agreement on a definition, there are several behavioral and cognitive characteristics generally attributed to entrepreneurs:

- They create or find opportunities to add value to the lives of customers by fulfilling a need(s) of those customers (Drucker, 1985; Christensen & Raynor, 2003; Sarasvathy, 2008).
- They innovate by assembling and organizing the financial, human, physical, and social capital required to take a product/service to the market that needs it (Schumpeter, 1991; Terry, 1995).
- They are catalytic leaders who create enterprises that learn from their failures and successes (Timmons & Spinelli, 2007).
- They are not deterred by the fact that they do not own the resources they require to achieve their goals; instead, they persuade others to contribute their resources to the enterprise via the strength of the entrepreneur's vision (Stevenson, 1983).
- They tolerate the risk necessary to engage in something new by learning how to effectively manage that risk (Antonites & Wordsworth, 2009).
- They have a goal of growth for their enterprise and for themselves. They seek to increase their reach (Lichtenstein & Lyons, 2010b).

While it is important to understand the kind of thinking and acting that underlies entrepreneurship, arguably, it is a particular type of entrepreneurship that is most relevant to this discussion—social entrepreneurship. Dees (1998: 3) contended that social entrepreneurship is "one species in the genus entrepreneurship." Social entrepreneurs exhibit the same characteristics noted for commercial entrepreneurs, but they do so in the service of a social mission that takes precedence

---

1 Portions of this chapter are excerpted with the permission of the Sol Price Center for Social Innovation from Lyons, T.S. (2016). "Leveraging Commercial and Social Entrepreneurship for the Revitalization of Marginalized Urban Communities," Framing Paper for the Panel on Social Entrepreneurship, *Activating Markets for Social Change Conference*, Los Angeles, CA: Sol Price Center for Social Innovation, Price School of Public Policy, University of Southern California (April 15).

DOI 10.1515/9781547400461-004

over all else, including the generation of profit, and they are highly accountable to stakeholders, including society, and not merely shareholders (Dees, 1998). In economic terms, they bring social goods to a market in need.

Social entrepreneurship is not solely the purview of nonprofit organizations, nor is it exclusive to for profit enterprises pursuing a double (economic and social) or triple (economic, environmental, and social) bottom line. Legal or organizational structure does not define social entrepreneurship (Austin, 2006; Kickul & Lyons, 2016). This means that social entrepreneurs can be found in the nonprofit, public and private sectors, and sometimes these entrepreneurs create enterprises that combine the best features of these various structures, known as "hybrids." The truly important distinction is that they think and act entrepreneurially, using markets responsibly, as they chase a social mission.

The principal goal of entrepreneurship is to generate economic wealth (Lichtenstein & Lyons, 2010a). Entrepreneurs try to create wealth for themselves and their families by creating a business asset, which is sustainable and can be transferred from generation to generation. There is nothing inherently wrong with creating wealth, as long as the opportunity to do so is available to everyone. It is the collective creation of wealth across the families of a community that ultimately yields the economic transformation of that community and the ability to eliminate the social problems that accompany a lack of wealth.

Unfortunately, in our world not everyone has the opportunity to create wealth (Oliver & Shapiro, 2006). This is true in places both rural and urban. It is caused by a lack of access to quality education, the globalization of the economy and its resultant shrinking of well-paying job opportunities, isolation (both economic and physical), immigration, and health issues, among other challenges (Silver & Bures, 1997; Durr & Lyons, 2000; Wang & Li, 2007; Yesudian, 2007; Lyons, et al, 2015). These problems were produced, in part, by the over-concentration of wealth in the hands of a few and serve to perpetuate it.

Over the course of our history, some governments have attempted to address this issue by adopting redistributive policies and programs; and yet, the problems persist and the wealth gap grows. While these efforts are well intentioned, they are not systemic and, therefore, do not have the power to transform. Instead of perfecting markets, in some cases, they have unintentionally destroyed those same markets (Lichtenstein & Lyons, 2010b).

If what we are doing currently is not working, then what will? Fostering responsible capitalism through entrepreneurship is one answer to this question. This can, and should, happen on two levels:

1. Through the efforts of individual commercial entrepreneurs in low-income communities

2. Through the work of social entrepreneurs in support of those commercial entrepreneurs

As noted above, if properly motivated, individual commercial entrepreneurs are given the opportunity to start, grow, and sustain their own enterprises, they can generate economic wealth for themselves and their families. This, in turn, can result in community-wide wealth creation, if this wealth creation effort is implemented systemically, systematically, and strategically. This latter caveat is crucial.

The place to start is by acknowledging that to be successful in this endeavor, we can not conflate entrepreneurship and self-employment. At best, most self-employed businesspeople in our communities are what the Global Entrepreneurship Monitor project calls "necessity entrepreneurs." This term refers to people who start businesses only because they perceive themselves as having no other economic options. Thus, their businesses are economically marginal, providing only basic necessities to the owners and their families. While this is important, it is not enough to create the level of surplus necessary to permitting the savings and investment essential for wealth creation. Considering this, it is little wonder that some scholars have identified self-employment as a cause of economic inequality (Silver and Bures, 1997). Our focus needs to be on fostering entrepreneurs, who are innovating by bringing something new to the market or reaching underserved markets and who seek to grow their businesses beyond the corner grocery, hair salon, or storefront restaurant.

However, this is where efforts to support entrepreneurship often go off the rails, reverting to approaches that in effect perpetuate the status quo and exacerbate wealth inequality. In many places, entrepreneurship is still viewed as an elitist activity, engaged in by serial entrepreneurs who are launching technology-based and venture capital-backed businesses. Investment decisions are made based on the perceived revenue generation capability of the business in question and whether the entrepreneur has the immediate capability to successfully lead the business. Governments take their cues from venture capitalists and invest in this low-hanging entrepreneurial fruit. After all, they, too, want to maximize their return on investment, in the form of jobs created and taxes generated. It should be no surprise that those who observe activities based on this very limited definition of entrepreneurship have argued that these activities exacerbate wealth inequality by greatly enriching those who participate (Isenberg, 2014).

What this approach fails to recognize is that entrepreneurs do not come to entrepreneurship fully equipped to be successful. They get to that point through a long process of knowledge acquisition, experience, and feedback from coaches and mentors (Kutzhanova et al., 2009). In other words, they get to the mastery of their craft through skill building (Lichtenstein & Lyons, 2010b; Lyons & Lyons,

2015; Neck et al., 2018). Thus, current public and private investors in entrepreneurship are essentially "cherry picking" the most skilled entrepreneurs without investing in producing more cherries. This may be good for them, in the form of financial and political pay-off in the short run, but it is not healthy for society in the long run. It perpetuates wealth inequality by limiting the number of people who can participate in, and reap the benefits of, entrepreneurship.

Elsewhere, we have argued that today's low-income urban "necessity" entrepreneur could become highly successful, if they receive assistance in building her skills so that she can move her company forward (Lyons, 2015). This requires an investment in this entrepreneur by the community over time. It is not an investment in her current enterprise, which may or may not have high revenue-generating potential. It is an investment in the development of her skillset as an entrepreneur, which, in turn, will ultimately allow her to build a highly successful business (Lichtenstein & Lyons, 2010b).

As an example, an entrepreneur in the United States might start by opening a small, storefront Mexican restaurant. This business likely only generates enough revenue to keep a roof over the heads of the entrepreneur's family and food on the table and would not be considered by most people to be investment worthy. However, this entrepreneur is fortunate enough to live in a community that supports a coaching system designed to help properly motivated entrepreneurs to develop their skills. After about a year of working with her coach, the entrepreneur recognizes that the tamales she sells in her restaurant are attracting people from other communities to her establishment. Feeling empowered by her growing entrepreneurial skills, she proposes that she launch a new business that manufactures her tamales and sells them throughout the region and, ultimately, the country. Her coach helps her through this process.

This necessity entrepreneur has become a growth-focused (opportunity) entrepreneur with an enterprise that is attractive to private investment. She now has a business that is a wealth-creating asset. This example is based on a true story and illustrates how a public investment in human development that focuses on providing an opportunity to a low-income individual to pursue entrepreneurship can be a first step toward shrinking the wealth inequality gap.

Social Entrepreneurs Supporting the Efforts of Low-Income Commercial Entrepreneurs

To this point, we have discussed the power of commercial entrepreneurship to generate individual and community wealth within low-income communities. However, as the preceding example suggests, this requires investment by communities in efforts to facilitate this. Furthermore, these efforts must intentionally expand the opportunity afforded by entrepreneurship to more people. This is where social entrepreneurship comes into play.

We suggest that those organizations—nonprofit, private, and public—that provide business, financial, and technical assistance to entrepreneurs in a responsible and equitable way, with a goal of improving the economy for all, are acting as social entrepreneurs. The community-based entrepreneurship coaching program alluded to in the example above would be one illustration of this. As was noted in Chapter 3, fostering entrepreneurship is ultimately about developing entrepreneurs so that they, in turn, have the capability to develop their businesses. It is a form of human capital development before business development. When the focus is placed on individual people rather than the organizations they create and lead, new opportunities to effect change present themselves. Human capability underlies success in any endeavor. Entrepreneurship is no exception.

If we accept this premise, then where do social entrepreneurs begin in their efforts to foster commercial entrepreneurship as a means of addressing wealth inequality? Lichtenstein and Lyons (2010b) have suggested that the most effective way to build entrepreneurship capability is to begin by segmenting the market of entrepreneurs to be assisted. They argue that the most useful way to do this is by the skill level of the entrepreneur. There is a set of essential skills that are universal to successful entrepreneurship, no matter the entrepreneur's geographic location, ethnicity, gender, income level, religious beliefs, etc. While these contextual factors are important, when it comes to success at entrepreneurship, they are secondary to the requisite "hard" and "soft" skills of this profession. Hard skills are the basic skills of business: accounting, finance, marketing, operations management, and so forth. Soft skills include creativity, people management, and resilience, to name a few (Lyons & Lyons, 2015).

The ability to segment entrepreneurs by skill level hinges on being able to identify the essential skills of successful entrepreneurship and measure them in a clinical way. Lyons and Lyons (2015) have developed a tool for doing this, called the Readiness Inventory for Successful Entrepreneurship (RISE). RISE is a Web-based skill assessment tool that has its foundation in a theory of measurement developed by Dr. John S. Lyons at the University of Chicago called Communimetrics (Lyons, 2009). Unlike the reigning theory of measurement, psychometrics, Communimetrics is clinical, not predictive. Rather than attempting to answer the question, "Who will be a successful entrepreneur?" it addresses the question "How skilled are you as an entrepreneur at this given point in time?"

RISE measures thirty essential skills for entrepreneurship success identified through a systematic literature review and field research with entrepreneurs and ESOs. Four skill domains organize these individual skills:

1. Business Management Skills – the skills essential to managing the structures of business (hard skills)
2. Organizational Process Skills – the skills essential to managing the processes of business (hard skills)
3. Relationship Management Skills – the skills essential to managing people within and outside of the business (soft skills)
4. Transformation Management Skills – the skills essential to managing change (soft skills)

Because of its Communimetric base, RISE provides meaningful measures at the individual skill level, the domain level, and overall. A baseline can be set, and changes over time can be tracked. Placing individual entrepreneurs at an overall skill level permits the efficient and effective matching of assistance to the specific capability of the given entrepreneur, ensuring that the individual is ready to use the assistance offered (Lichtenstein & Lyons, 2010b). The relationship between the assistance intervention and its impact on skill improvement can be determined as well.

Skills are applied knowledge. Skill development requires both the acquisition of knowledge and practicing that knowledge in the field (Baron & Henry, 2010; Kutzhanova et al., 2009). Therefore, merely providing training, classroom education, or expert advice is not enough. Entrepreneurs need the opportunity to engage in what Coyle (2009) calls "deep practice." This involves practice that is intentional and strategic in its focus, requires the entrepreneur to leave her or his comfort zone, is intensive (Coyle suggests 10,000 hours to achieve skill mastery), and receives regular feedback. This latter prescription is particularly important.

Practicing without feedback as to the appropriateness and quality of that practice might yield no progress in skill development or, worse yet, the establishment of bad habits. However, if there is a knowledgeable person present who can help the entrepreneur to identify her or his errors and to make changes that improve their practice, skills can be developed and ultimately mastered. In our experience, the best person to provide this regular feedback is a coach.

Coaches can interact with entrepreneurs in two important ways: personal (individual coaching) and peer group coaching (Kutzhanova et al., 2009). Personal coaching involves a one-on-one relationship between the entrepreneur and the coach in which the coach is helping the entrepreneur to acknowledge their skill weaknesses and putting the entrepreneur into situations that force the latter to take responsibility for their own skill development through asking probing questions, providing field experiences, and other interventions. An illustration of how this works comes from an intervention by a coach in a coaching system established by one of the authors and a colleague in the southern United States. In this example, the coach is working with an entrepreneur named Gary (not his real name) who is a cabinetmaker, starting his own business. One of Gary's identified skill weaknesses is his inability to engage in the "hard" skill of job costing. Gary has been getting by charging a lump sum fee for his work, based on his own internal calculations. His coach has been trying to convince him that learning how to be more accurate about what he charges will greatly enhance his business. This effort is going nowhere; so, the coach decides that a field trip is in order. The coach takes Gary to a local big box hardware retailer. As they are walking from the parking lot to the door, the coach tells Gary that he wants a cabinet for his home, and he gives him some specifications on size and style. Inside the store, the coach suggests that Gary find all the materials he will need to build this cabinet and record each item separately, along with its price. When Gary completes this task, the coach asks him to tally these costs. The coach then asks Gary what he has in his hand. Gary replies that he has an itemized list of the supplies he will need to build the cabinet, along with their cost. The coach says, "Good. Now, what are you worth, Gary?" Gary looks at him blankly. The coach says, "What is the time it will take you to build the cabinet worth?" They discuss the number of hours required and what Gary feels is a fair per-hour price for his time. Gary then makes this calculation, and the coach asks him to add the cost of time to the cost of materials. "Now what do you have?" asks the coach. Gary replies, "The total cost of the job." "Exactly," says the coach, "Now you don't have to guess as to the cost of building a cabinet."

As if this was not enough reinforcement of Gary's new skill, the manager of the store approaches them, tells them that he has been watching them for a while, and wants to know what they are doing. When they explain, the manager says to Gary, "That's great that you have this kind of support as you build your business. As it happens, the guy who builds cabinets for our kitchen renovation team quit yesterday, would you like the contract?"

Peer group coaching involves putting together a group of 8–12 entrepreneurs who are all at the same skill level. The coach then acts as a facilitator of their discussions. The entrepreneurs are involved in setting their own agenda. They act as an advisory board to each other, sharing insights, information, and experiences. They also serve as a support group to each other, as entrepreneurship can sometimes be a very lonely undertaking (Kutzhanova et al., 2009).

Assembling a peer group like this would not be possible without a tool like the RISE to classify entrepreneurs by their skill level. Similarly, in the example of personal coaching, Gary's coach was able strategically to identify his skill weakness using a tool that was the forerunner to the RISE. As several pilot projects have demonstrated, a combination of assessing entrepreneurship skills and using that assessment to guide coaching interventions can be a very effective way to develop entrepreneurs (Kutzhanova et al., 2009).

Thus, developing entrepreneurs by addressing their skills is a useful strategy that social entrepreneurs can adopt for enhancing commercial entrepreneurship in their communities. It recognizes that entrepreneurship can be pursued by anyone with the proper motivation, and it provides useful assistance to those that want to make the journey. This strategy appropriately connects learning and practice to the wealth building power of entrepreneurship and makes this more widely available.

As entrepreneurs become more skilled, they have the capacity to restructure their enterprises in a way that allows the latter to move more efficiently and effectively through the stages of the business life cycle (Lichtenstein & Lyons, 2010b). Ultimately, this is how wealth is created. A business that stays at a very early growth stage may generate some income for its owner, but it does not generate wealth. The latter is only possible when the enterprise grows to a stage where it is generating enough revenue to allow the owner to save and invest, either back into the business or in other assets.

How does a social entrepreneur who supports commercial entrepreneurship as a community wealth-building activity know where a given enterprise is in its life cycle or when it moves to another stage? Lichtenstein and Lyons (2008) have created a development-oriented business life cycle stage model that makes this possible. Unlike standard life cycle stage models, which focus on attempting to predict how quickly an enterprise will move from start-up to high growth, the Lichtenstein and Lyons model is more concerned with mapping the growth of the enterprise. This permits the enterprise development social entrepreneur to intervene strategically at a given life cycle stage to aid the entrepreneur in moving the business forward.

This is possible because this model places clear parameters on its six stages (see Figure 4.1). It is very clear where one stage ends and the next begins. The six stages of the model are preventure, existence or infancy, early growth, expansion or sustained growth, maturity, and decline (Lichtenstein & Lyons, 2008). From a wealth building and economic development perspective, expansion or sustained growth and maturity are the target stages. Early growth is the "crossroads" stage, where the entrepreneur must decide between operating a necessity or life style business and actively pursuing growth. If a community, or society, seeks to foster wealth creation to combat wealth inequality, it must nudge more entrepreneurs toward the latter choice. The best way to do this is by empowering them through support in building their skills, which yields self-efficacy, as in the case of the restaurateur cum tamale manufacturer discussed earlier in this chapter.

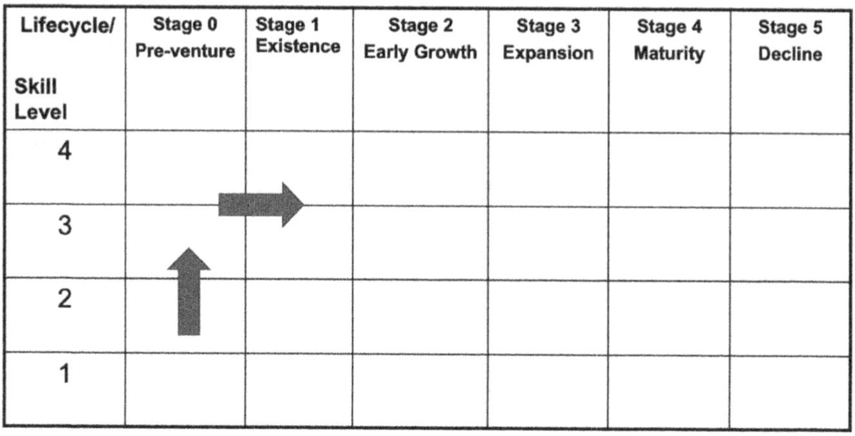

Lifecycle/ Skill Level	Stage 0 Pre-venture	Stage 1 Existence	Stage 2 Early Growth	Stage 3 Expansion	Stage 4 Maturity	Stage 5 Decline
4						
3						
2						
1						

Source: Adapted from Lichtenstein, G. A., & Lyons, T.S. (2010). Investing in entrepreneurs: A strategic approach for strengthening your regional and community economy. Santa Barbara, CA: Praeger/ABC-CLIO.

Figure 4.1: The Pipeline of Entrepreneurs and Enterprises

In their book, *Investing in Entrepreneurs*, Lichtenstein and Lyons (2010b) put the variables entrepreneurship skill and stage in the business life cycle together to create a conceptual model they call the "pipeline of entrepreneurs and enterprises" (see Figure 4.1). This pipeline is useful to social entrepreneur ESOs because it allows them to "map" the enterprises in their community or region in a way that permits strategic assistance. They can tailor solutions and allocate scarce resources that are appropriate to the skill level of the entrepreneur and the life cycle stage of the enterprise. In this way, they can manage the volume and flow of the pipeline, helping to increase the quantity and quality of the local entrepreneurial pool (Lichtenstein & Lyons, 2010b).

The keys to fostering entrepreneurship in a way that enables broader wealth creation include:
- Acknowledge that, at its essence, entrepreneurship is about creating wealth, which is a good thing if everyone has access to the opportunity to do so.
- Take a "big tent" approach to entrepreneurship: anyone who is properly motivated can learn and participate. Adopt the perspective that entrepreneurs can be developed. Success rests with the mastery of a skill set. These skills can be identified, taught, and practiced.

–   Put the entrepreneur ahead of the enterprise. A skilled entrepreneur can take their enterprise through its life cycle efficiently and effectively.
–   Create an environment at the community/regional level that is supportive of entrepreneurship at all levels of skill.
–   Encourage and support "necessity entrepreneurs" in becoming "opportunity entrepreneurs."

In the ensuing chapters, we will discuss and examine several examples of efforts to support entrepreneurship that address wealth inequality in some way.

References

Antonites, A.J., & Wordsworth, R. (2009). Risk tolerance: A perspective on entrepreneurship education. *Southern African Business Review* 13 (3): 69–85.

Austin, J. (2006). Three avenues for social entrepreneurship research. In J. Mair, J. Robinson, & Hockerts, K. (Eds.). *Social entrepreneurship* (pp. 22–33). New York: Palgrave Macmillan.

Baron, R.A., & Henry, R.A. (2010). How entrepreneurs acquire the capacity to excel: Insights from research on expert performance. *Strategic Entrepreneurship Journal* 4: 49–65.

Christensen, C.M., & Raynor, M.E. (2003). *The innovator's solution: Creating and sustaining Successful growth.* Boston, MA: Harvard Business School Press.

Coyle, D. (2009). *The talent code.* New York: Bantam.

Dees, J.G. (1998). The meaning of "social entrepreneurship." Palo Alto, CA: Graduate School of Business, Stanford University. Retrieved from http://www.caseatduke.org/documents/Dees_sedef.pdf.

Drucker, P.F. (1985). Innovation and entrepreneurship: Practice and principals. New York: Harper & Row.

Durr, M., Lyons, T.S., & Lichtenstein, G.A. (2000). Identifying the unique needs of urban entrepreneurs. *Race and Society* 3: 75–90.

Isenberg, D. (2014). Entrepreneurship always leads to inequality. *Harvard Business Review*, March 10.

Kickul, J., & Lyons, T.S. (2016). *Understanding social entrepreneurship: The relentless pursuit of mission in an ever changing world*, Second Edition. New York: Routledge.

Kutzhanova, N., Lyons, T.S., & Lichtenstein, G.A. (2009). Skill-based development of entrepreneurs and the role of personal and peer group coaching in enterprise development. *Economic Development Quarterly* 23 (3): 193–210.

Lichtenstein, G.A., & Lyons, T.S. (2008). Revisiting the business life cycle: Proposing an actionable model for assessing and fostering entrepreneurship. *International Journal of Entrepreneurship and Innovation* 9 (4): 241–250.

Lyons, T.S., & Lichtenstein, G.A. (2010a). A community-wide framework for encouraging social entrepreneurship using the pipeline of entrepreneurs and enterprises model. In A. Fayolle & H. Matlay (Eds.). *Handbook of research on social entrepreneurship.* Cheltenham, UK: Edward Elgar: 252–270.

Lichtenstein, G.A., & Lyons, T.S. (2010b). *Investing in entrepreneurs: A strategic approach for strengthening your regional and community economy.* Santa Barbara, CA: Praeger/ABC-CLIO.

Lyons, J.S. (2009). *Communimetrics: A communications theory of measurement in human service settings*. New York: Springer.

Lyons, T.S. (2015). Entrepreneurship and community development: What matters and why? *Community Development* 46 (5): 456–460.

Lyons, T.S., & Lyons, J.S. (2015). *A skills assessment approach to operationalizing entrepreneur skills theory*. White paper. Morristown, NJ: Lyons Entrepreneurial Assessment Partners, LLC.

Lyons, T.S., Rogoff, E.G., Dean, M., & Marks, S. (2015). *How entrepreneurship service organizations can better serve immigrant entrepreneurs*. Working Paper, New York: Lawrence N. Field Center for Entrepreneurship, Baruch College, City University of New York.

Neck, H.M., Neck, C.P., & Murray, E.L. (2018). *Entrepreneurship: The practice and mindset*. Los Angeles, CA: Sage.

Oliver, M.L., & Shapiro, T. (2006). *Black wealth, white wealth: A new perspective on racial inequality*. New York: Routledge.

Sarasvathy, S.D. (2008). *Effectuation: Elements of entrepreneurial expertise*. Cheltenham, UK: Edward Elgar.

Schumpeter, J. (1991). Comments on a plan for the study of entrepreneurship. In R. Swedberg (Ed.). *Joseph A. Schumpeter: The economics and sociology of capitalism* (pp. 406–428). Princeton, NJ: Princeton University Press.

Silver, H., & Bures, R. (1997). Dual cities? Sectoral shifts and metropolitan income inequality, 1980–90. *The Service Industries Journal* 17 (1): 69–90.

Stevenson, H.H. (1983). *A perspective on entrepreneurship*. Harvard Business School Working Paper 9–384–131.

Terry, J.V. (1995). *Dictionary for business finance* (3rd ed.). Fayetteville: University of Arkansas Press.

Timmons, J., & Spinelli, S. (2007). *New venture creation: Entrepreneurship for the 21st century*. New York: McGraw-Hill/Irwin

Wang, Q., & Li, W. (2007). Entrepreneurship, ethnicity and local contexts: Hispanic entrepreneurs in three U.S. southern metropolitan areas. *GeoJournal* 68 (2–3): 167–182.

Yesudian, C.A.K. (2007). Poverty alleviation programmes in India: A social audit. *Indian Journal of Medical Research* 126 (October): 364–373.

Chapter 5
An Example from New York City:
Competition THRIVE

The case study that follows provides one example of how wealth inequality can be addressed through entrepreneurship.[1] It tells the story of a collaborative effort by city government, a private foundation and a public institution of higher education to encourage business creation by immigrants living in New York City's economically disadvantaged neighborhoods. The interesting twist to this story is that the program described is aimed at building the capability and capacity of the social entrepreneurs who help the immigrant entrepreneurs in these neighborhoods to build wealth for themselves and their communities.

From 2011 to 2014, under sponsorship from the New York City Economic Development Corporation and the Deutsche Bank Americas Foundation, the Lawrence N. Field Center for Entrepreneurship at Baruch College ran three cycles of a competition, called Competition THRIVE, to develop innovative community-based programs that would foster and support entrepreneurship in targeted immigrant communities in New York City. Competition THRIVE reached out to local entrepreneurship support organizations (ESOs) to solicit innovative ideas and then provided financial and technical support for a pilot program. Based on the quality of the program ideas, the results of the pilots, and program revisions made and business plans developed based on learnings from the pilot period, a panel of judges from various organizations that intersect with the process of locally based immigrant entrepreneurship development chose winners and awarded funding that would support a full roll-out of the local groups' programs.

Competition THRIVE represents an innovative approach to supporting the process of immigrant entrepreneurship development through a business plan competition targeted to ESOs. This chapter reviews the circumstances that led to the development of the program, explains how the competition was administered and engaged various groups, highlights how the program was impactful, and details how lessons learned from the first cycle of the competition were applied in the second and third cycles.

Ultimately, this case study seeks to identify and detail a potentially replicable model for fostering community economic development that is focused on immi-

---

1 A portion of the chapter has been reprinted by permission. Lyons, T.S., Rogoff, E.G., & Dean, M. (2018). How entrepreneurship support organizations can better serve immigrant entrepreneurs. *American Journal of Entrepreneurship* 10 (1): 56–90.

DOI 10.1515/9781547400461-005

grant entrepreneurship. It explores approaches to overcoming shortcomings in the current practice of nongovernmental organizations that strive to help immigrant entrepreneurs by building partnerships among economic development agencies, corporate funders, academic entrepreneurship programs, and local immigrant-focused nonprofits. Finally, it furthers the discussion about the value of the business plan competition as a tool to educate entrepreneurs.

Background

Several recent studies have shown that first- and second-generation immigrants are among the United States' most active entrepreneurs (Liu, 2012; Hart & Acs, 2011; Tienda & Raijman, 2004). Immigrants constitute 21 percent of this country's self-employed. In New York City, immigrants make up almost 38 percent of the population, 46 percent of the labor force, and 53 percent of the total self-employed (U.S. Census Bureau, 2012). The outsized role of immigrants on entrepreneurial activity is broadly seen. Data from the Kauffman Index: Start-Up Activity reports that immigrants are twice as likely as native-born Americans to be entrepreneurs (Jackson, 2015). A report by the New American Economy estimated that there are nearly six million immigrant-owned businesses in the United States and that immigrants or their children founded over 40 percent of Fortune 500 firms (New American Economy, 2016). *Inc.* magazine reported that between 1995 and 2005 immigrants founded 52 percent of all new Silicon Valley businesses (Bluestein, 2017).

Yet, the path to successful entrepreneurship for immigrants is littered with obstacles. Many of these are what Lichtenstein and Lyons (1996: 30) have called "transaction barriers"—these are non-financial problems with acquiring resources. These include challenges of language, differing culturally based mores and expectations, a lack of understanding of new legal and financial systems and no credit history (Bowles & Colton, 2007). Other obstacles facing immigrant entrepreneurs involve the lack of networks essential to conducting business—financing networks, distribution channels, and so forth. The lack of a strong system of networks has caused some immigrant groups to attempt to replicate these networks in their own enclaves, which, while being sometimes beneficial in the short term, may actually perpetuate physical and economic isolation (Durr et al., 2000) resulting in a financial penalty to these entrepreneurs in the form of lost revenue due to heavy reliance on a co-ethnic market (Shinnar et al., 2011).

These obstacles to immigrant entrepreneurship are challenging, but they can be overcome with help. Intermediary organizations, often referred to as entrepreneurship support organizations, provide this assistance. ESOs can be found in most communities. They may be private, public or nonprofit in their legal structure, but they are most often organized as not-for-profit entities. Their chief function is to provide technical and/or financial assistance to entrepreneurs to help them start, grow, and sustain their businesses.

ESOs take many forms; among these are Small Business Development Centers (SBDCs), business incubators, micro-lending and micro-enterprise programs, neighborhood economic development corporations, community development financial institutions (CDFIs), SCORE chapters, Boots2Business (B2B), and business outreach centers (BOCs), to name only a few. They offer training, counseling, office space, access to basic business services, and financing, among other services (Heriot et al., 2017). Most of these organizations make their services available to all entrepreneurs in their catchment areas. For some, the fact that they are in predominantly immigrant communities automatically means their focus will most likely be on immigrant entrepreneurship. For others, this is an emerging specialization brought about by increased public interest and support for this segment of entrepreneurship. Either way, in the process of supporting business development, these ESOs help immigrant entrepreneurs overcome the transaction barriers and the networking challenges noted above.

Due to the importance of immigrant entrepreneurship to the U.S. economy and the key role of ESOs in helping these entrepreneurs succeed, the related questions of how effective the ESOs are at helping these immigrant entrepreneurs prosper and how they might become more effective are important to examine. While little or no research has been conducted regarding the formal assistance of immigrant entrepreneurs, literature exploring general ESO efficacy has emerged over the past decade or so. While some researchers question the quality of specific types of ESO studies (Gu et al., 2008), the consensus seems to be that ESOs, while helpful, are not nearly as effective and efficient as they could be in providing help to their client entrepreneurs. More specifically, a review of this literature reveals the following shortcomings of the current approach by ESOs (Curran, 2000; Sullivan, 2000; Aldrich & Martinez, 2001; Lichtenstein & Lyons, 2001; Kayne, 2002; DeFaoite et al., 2003; Henry et al., 2003; Lichtenstein et al., 2004; Boter & Lundstrom, 2005; Lichtenstein & Lyons, 2010):

1. Supply driven service delivery; not demand driven service delivery
2. An over-emphasis on service delivery as opposed to development
3. An over-emphasis on the business at the expense of the entrepreneur
4. A limited focus on innovation
5. A lack of business entrepreneurship acumen
6. A lack of business acumen
7. Limited economic impact
8. A lack of "successful practice" knowledge

All of this suggests that an intervention is needed to help ESOs become more innovative, more responsive to client entrepreneurs' needs, better focused, more effective, and more sustainable. This is no less true for ESOs that serve immigrant entrepreneurs, whose needs are at once broader in the sense that they must cover a full array of business issues, and more specific in that they must deal with rather specialized questions such as those pertaining to immigration. Such an intervention must be both creative and innovative. It must capture the attention of ESOs, offer them incentive to participate, and foster in them the same kinds of thinking and acting expected of their client entrepreneurs. Moreover, by involving other organizations that can provide funding, entrepreneurship expertise, and business networking, shortcomings of the ESOs can be addressed.

One such intervention is the business plan competition. The business plan competition has been employed as a teaching tool by entrepreneurship programs in business schools for many years. While there is some debate about whether business plans are essential to the success of young companies (Shane & Delmar, 2004; Lange et al., 2007; Brinckmann et al., 2009), there is a broad consensus that business plan competitions offer several benefits to the entrepreneurs who participate in them. Among these are entrepreneurship skill building (including business management, risk management, leadership, teamwork and communication), access to beneficial networks, free mentoring or consulting advice, an opportunity for reflection on performance, sense-making, and confidence building (Hurst, 2000; Byrne, 2002; Chao-Tung & Yi Wen, 2007; Russell et al., 2008; Jones & Jones, 2011; Thomas et al, 2014; Watson et al., 2015). Zimmerman (2012) found business plans help entrepreneurship students to integrate effectively the various substantive aspects of business. Hallam et al. (2014) argue that competitions are more effective when they are part of a more holistic effort to immerse students in entrepreneurship and that the interdisciplinary diversity of competing teams is crucial to the effectiveness of the experience.

Typically, business plan competitions have been the purview of business schools, with a focus on developing student entrepreneurs and their businesses. The traditional model entails students creating a plan supported by mentors, ending with a presentation, which includes a question and answer period with judges. Most competitions award a cash prize and/or further technical support.

A newer trend has seen the use of this tool to stimulate entrepreneurial thinking and innovation among public policy makers and among early-stage entrepreneurs internationally (Funkhouser, 2012; McKenzie, 2015). Many business plan competitions at universities around the world now include tracks that encourage social entrepreneurship among students, including those from fields other than business (Kickul & Lyons, 2016). Despite this, there is still a need for more research into the efficacy of business plan competitions as a public policy tool aimed at fostering entrepreneurship (Schwartz et al., 2013). A unique approach to this kind of policy intervention is illustrated by the case of Competition THRIVE, which affords a vehicle for beginning to explore what might be effective in this arena.

The Case of Competition THRIVE

The New York City Economic Development Corporation (NYCEDC) functions as a semi-autonomous agency and is the City's primary vehicle for promoting economic growth in each of the five boroughs. NYCEDC's mission is to stimulate growth through expansion and redevelopment programs that encourage investment, generate prosperity, and strengthen the City's competitive position. NYCEDC serves as an advocate to the business community by building relationships with companies that allow them to take advantage of New York City's many opportunities. In 2010, NYCEDC began developing ideas for a program to stimulate entrepreneurship in immigrant communities through a vehicle such as the NESTA-style competition (the United Kingdom's National Endowment for Science, Technology and the Arts competition designed to stimulate and support community-led responses to climate change).

Simultaneously, because of research and conversations with community organizations and policy thought leaders (in particular, the Center for an Urban Future), Deutsche Bank Americas Foundation (DBAF) began a set of strategic conversations focused on grant making to initiatives supporting immigrant entrepreneurs. In late 2010, DBAF connected with NYCEDC to discuss their shared motivation of supporting immigrant entrepreneurs. NYCEDC shared that they were in the early stages of putting together a program structured as a business plan competition, and DBAF was immediately intrigued by it.

The DBAF is the New York City–based philanthropic arm of Deutsche Bank, a financial services firm with 98,000 employees located around the world and a growing presence in the United States. DBAF works in tandem with the Bank's Global Social Investment group to use the Bank's social financing expertise and investment banking skills, to support high-impact interventions that benefit low-income communities. DBAF's geographic focus is primarily New York City, in alignment with the Bank's obligations under the Community Reinvestment Act (CRA), which is the regulatory framework that requires banks to serve the credit needs of low-income communities in their assessment area.

In New York City, DBAF makes grants with a focus on affordable housing, education, and community economic development. The staff at DBAF is disciplined in deploying scarce philanthropic resources through targeted programmatic strategies that are defined following extensive research and conversations with stakeholders. These stakeholders include public sector agencies, community-based organizations, policy and advocacy thought partners, co-funders, and conventional capital providers.

A focus on immigrant entrepreneurs had a particular resonance for an international firm like Deutsche Bank. New York City's density and concentration of talent attracts big global firms like Deutsche Bank, and immigrants come here for the same reason: to find opportunity and start up new businesses. DBAF has always recognized that it is crucial that the places where the Bank does business and where its employees live be thriving communities with social opportunity, and immigrant communities seemed to have enormous potential for strengthening and diversifying the City's economy. Nonetheless, as noted previously, immigrant entrepreneurs face unique challenges: lack of access to credit, less formalized business skills, and language barriers.

DBAF presumed that joining forces with NYCEDC around a business plan competition would enable them to establish relationships quickly and source ideas from a range of organizations: micro-lenders, credit unions, and small business support organizations. Furthermore, with a limited philanthropic budget, DBAF was trying to identify market-based opportunities where a significant, time-limited philanthropic investment would establish a sustainable social business that could earn revenue and become self-sufficient without ongoing subsidy.

DBAF and NYCEDC quickly saw that a partnership would enable each party to leverage their resources and expertise. Agreeing to the importance of this issue, the two sides forged a plan to execute a competition among community-based organizations (CBOs). DBAF committed $105,000 and NYCEDC contributed $200,000 to fund the program. In 2011, the partnership between NYCEDC and DBAF was announced and NYCEDC issued a formal Request for Proposals (RFP) for a consultant to administer Competition THRIVE. The Lawrence N. Field Center for Entrepreneurship at Baruch College responded to the RFP from NYCEDC seeking a qualified organization to run Competition THRIVE and won the contract. The staff at NYCEDC reported that Baruch's expertise in the areas of entrepreneurship development programs and immigrant entrepreneurship were important factors in awarding Baruch the contract.

Competition THRIVE Years 1, 2, and 3

Competition Goals

The goals of the program as stated in the RFP calling for proposals from local CBOs were as follows:

1. Help small businesses go to scale.
2. Explore new methods for assisting sectors of entrepreneurial communities that are unable to expand capacity.
3. Advance the initiative to increase accessibility of city-sponsored business assistance and subsidy programs to immigrant populations.
4. Promote innovation at the grassroots level by leveraging public and foundation assets with entrant groups (organizations that submit proposals).
5. Strengthen partnerships between entrants and the New York City government.
6. Provide opportunities for neighborhood-based not-for-profit organizations to expand capacity for new and financially self-sustaining program development and implementation.

Competition Structure

Competition THRIVE had a program length of approximately one year. The Competition was divided into four distinct phases and starts with the Notice-to-Proceed and ends with a final awards ceremony. Below is a list of the phases (some run concurrently) and the major tasks that fell within those designated periods.

Timeline

– Phase 1—Precompetition (one month)
– Phase 2—Round 0 (three months)
– Phase 3—Round I (eight months)
– Phase 4—Round II (two months)

Precompetition

After the receipt of the Notice-to-Proceed, the Consultant (Field Center for Entrepreneurship) and NYCEDC entered the precomputation phase. At the kickoff meeting, the Field Center and NYCEDC agreed to administrative requirements including, but not limited to, a recommended scheduling tool, frequency and reporting methodology, project status reports and meeting minute requirements, payment procedures and other project management tools.

A mailing list of possible entrants was created (which was continuously updated for the subsequent cycles). The list included nonprofit organizations (providing technical assistance, advocacy services, capacity building and support for entrepreneurship) from all five New York City boroughs—Bronx, Brooklyn, Manhattan, Queens, and Staten Island. These organizations could either be currently supporting immigrant entrepreneurs, looking to expand their reach to support immigrant entrepreneurs, or looking to reach additional immigrant communities. This list also included foundations, credit unions, chambers of commerce, banks, consulates, trade unions, labor unions, local politicians, immigrant media outlets, etc. Marketing materials included a self-mailer, e-mail, and a webpage. To streamline the receipt of entrant proposals, a designated email address was used as well as a designated telephone number for all inquiries.

Round 0

Round 0 began with a promotional material mass mailing, which coincided with a press release and the webpage launch. Marketing and promotion continued throughout this phase and individual calls were made to high priority targets. A single point of contact was designated to handle all inquiries whether by e-mail or phone. During this phase, criteria for the proposed pilot program was developed and communicated to potential entrants at a public information session that included a question and answer period. Potential entrants were informed that the judges would be looking for proposals with the following characteristics— innovative and creative, feasible, scalable, implementable, and sustainable. For THRIVE 3, a panel discussion of prior winners' experiences in the Competition was added to the information session.

The pilot program three-page proposal requirements included the following:
- **Pilot Program Proposed**
    - o What is the key problem addressed? What immigrant population benefits?
    - o How is your pilot unique, innovative, and creative?
    - o Do other organizations provide this service? How is your service distinct?
    - o What are your unique strengths and capacities?
    - o Who are the key staff members that will manage the program/service (resumes in the Addendum)?
- **Pilot Program Budget**
    - o What resources (staff, capital, equipment, support) are needed to execute the pilot program?
    - o How will the $25,000 planning/implementation funds be used?
    - o How will the $100,000 award be used to scale the program?
- **Addendum**
    - o Information necessary to support proposal (annual report, audited financial statements, resumes of key staff, etc.)

Round I

During Round I, five finalists were selected and awarded $25,000 each to conduct pilot programs (over the course of six months) that were expected to inform the development of their business plan. Technical assistance (TA) was provided by a team of three (two professors and one program director—all from Baruch) who had expertise in community and economic development, finance, business modeling, and business plan development. All the finalists were expected to have TA meetings at least twice a month and complete three major milestones. Finalists had to determine what would be the desired outcome of their pilot and what would be their success metrics. They also had to submit a draft business plan in the fifth month and a final plan at the end of the sixth month.

Round II

During Round II, all finalists made a five-minute pitch to the judges followed by a five-minute question and answer period. Competition results were revealed at an awards ceremony followed up by a press release.

Judging

Seven judges were chosen and agreed upon by NYCEDC, DBAF, and Baruch College. Each year the composition of the judges changed except for spots reserved for NYEDC, a representative from Deutsche Bank and the Commissioner of the Mayor's Office for Immigrant Affairs. Qualifications for judges were as follows:
- Ability to reach consensus with a diverse group of stakeholders with unique opinions and perspectives
- Extensive experience in managerial/decision-making role
- Demonstrated leader in respective field
- Extensive experience working with some/all the following constituencies:
  o community-based organizations
  o immigrant communities
  o small business owners/entrepreneurs
- Expertise in one or all the following areas:
  o business development
  o financial management
  o financial technical assistance
  o familiarity with issues facing NYC's immigrant communities
  o management consulting
  o nonprofit management

During Round I, judges evaluated the entrants' pilot proposals on whether their program was a realistic, marketable idea that fulfilled a need that currently was unmet or not well satisfied. The proposed program had to be innovative and scalable and could be 1) a brand new service and/or product, 2) an improvement to an existing service and/or product, or 3) the unique adaptation of an existing service and/or product. The proposal was also required to make clear the social and economic needs the organization/firm primarily addressed, and how the pilot would become a viable and sustainable enterprise within a reasonable period.

For Round II, judges analyzed the five finalists' written business plans with an eye toward gauging the potential for the eventual launch of a viable program.

Judges evaluated plan potential based on the following criteria:
1. Program Pilot
   Each organization had to demonstrate that, during the six-month pilot, they had begun to execute a program, which clearly identified a target population, acknowledged a service delivery gap, and proposed a solution.
2. Organizational Capability/Capacity
   Given existing organizational capacity (skilled management team, equipment, facilities), would additional financial resources enable this organization to implement their proposed program?
3. Sustainability
   The organization had developed a viable revenue model and/or fundraising plan.
4. Impact/Scalability
   The organization had developed a program model, which could be replicated across communities and organizations across New York City. The proposed program aligned with Competition THRIVE's goal of increasing the success rate among NYC's immigrant entrepreneurial community.
5. Innovation
   The organization had developed a program that was innovative and creative.

Scoring was conducted using a 7-point Likert scale, ranging from (1) Strongly Disagree to (7) Strongly Agree.

The major differences in the judging criteria from the pilot proposal phase to the business plan phase included the scoring of how well the finalists integrated lessons learned into their pilot, their receptivity to technical assistance and how well they presented their plan and articulated answers.

Results

The first Competition was a success with the Queens Economic Development Corporation (QEDC) winning the $100,000 first prize for a Chinese language-training program for home improvement contractors to take the New York City Department of Consumer Affairs' licensing exam. They were also successful in getting the New York City Department of Consumer Affairs to offer the exam in Chinese.

DBAF was so pleased with the results of the Competition that they offered a $25,000 challenge grant to the competition runner-up, Business Outreach Center Network (Brooklyn-based micro-enterprise/small business development organization), contingent on their raising matching funds. Their project was the development of an *Impact Platform*, a scalable online resource and information system that builds on institutional knowledge and generates greater community impact. It is a web-based single point of access to all TA, training, and lending tools and resources for business counselors/lenders. Internally, it creates added efficiencies, building a scalable model for capacity building and community impact. Externally, the Platform enables staff to serve the needs of immigrant entrepreneurs at any place/time.

NYCEDC decided to repeat Competition THRIVE in 2012–2013 with Baruch College continuing in its position as program consultant. Some minor changes were made to the program with a new focus on seeking out *more innovative* approaches to serving immigrant entrepreneurs and extending eligibility requirements to include for-profit organizations. Western Union and the Garfield Foundation provided additional funding and two prizes were awarded. The community-based organization CAMBA Small Business Services won a $150,000 first prize for developing and conducting a course for immigrant and low-income entrepreneurs to use tablet-based technology to transform their cash-and-carry businesses into bankable businesses. A second prize of $75,000 was awarded to the New York Public Library, Science Industry and Business Library (SIBL) for developing a succession-training program for immigrant family-owned businesses and strategically collaborating with two library systems (Brooklyn and Queens Public Libraries).

For THRIVE Year 2, new language was added to the call for proposals to emphasize the NYCEDC's desire for *more innovative proposals*. Innovation with respect to the context of THRIVE was communicated as follows:
- New technological advances to support immigrant entrepreneurs
- New methods or processes to support immigrant entrepreneurs
- New strategic alliances or joint ventures to support immigrant entrepreneurs
- New strategies for reaching presently underserved immigrant entrepreneurs

These were characteristics that The NYCEDC did not feel were adequately represented among the Year 1 competitors. Adding a focus on innovation for THRIVE Year 2 resulted in three of the finalists piloting projects with a technology focus as opposed to only one for THRIVE Year 1.

For THRIVE Year 3, new language was added to the call for proposals and ESOs were encouraged to *collaborate* on a proposal submission. In previous cycles, it was believed that collaboration was acceptable; however, competition organizers did not want entrants to feel there was a bias; so, the language created merely stated that entrants who wished to collaborate could do so. Language regarding innovation with respect to the context of THRIVE was communicated as detailed above. For Year 3, there were two repeat finalists, BOC as a prime working with All Boroughs LLC, and QEDC as a subcontractor to the Urban Justice League. Three of the five finalists represented collaborations between two organizations. Two of the projects focused on facilitating a better connection between immigrant entrepreneurs and the construction sector, and one model submitted by an ESO called The Working World proposed worker-owned cooperatives. This latter organization had been successful in implementing this model in Argentina and was interested in bringing it to a community in the Rockaways section of Queens that was devastated by Hurricane Sandy. Another proposal, the eventual winner, proposed a buyer's cooperative for Latino restaurant owners from the South Bronx who were feeling threatened by new regulations, neighborhood gentrification and the influx of chain restaurants. In the end, four of the five finalists' projects were substantially more complex than any of the other projects previously seen in Years 1 or 2, reflecting the nature of the challenges met and the team approach to meeting them.

Impact on ESOs and their Client Immigrant Entrepreneurs

To ascertain the impact that Competition THRIVE has had on the capability of participating ESOs to serve immigrant entrepreneurs, the prizewinners for each of the three years of the competition were interviewed. In Year 1, QEDC was the competition winner and BOC was the first runner-up, each being awarded prize money. In Year 2, CAMBA and the New York Public Library each received prize money as the winner and first runner-up, respectively. In Year 3, only the winner received a prize. That was the South Bronx Overall Economic Development Corporation (SoBRO). Each of these prize-winners was asked to self-report the impact the competition had on their organization and its clients since receiving their award.

What follows is a summary of each first place ESO's report taken in chronological order. Each report includes a brief description of the ESO's innovative program/project, a discussion of their piloting effort, their impact on immigrant entrepreneur clients to date, and an accounting of what they believe were the keys to their success.

Year 1: QEDC—Home Improvement Contractor Training (HICT)—Winner

The HICT program provides a seamless, client-focused service (in immigrant participant's language) to help them become licensed. Through a training program, follow-up one-on-one consultations, guest speakers, and trips to the NYC Department of Consumer Affairs' (DCA) licensing department for examination, the client receives all the necessary guidance to become licensed and apply better business practices.

Pilot—The pilot included eighty-three participants, training four groups to take the DCA licensing exam in Chinese. Of the participants, sixty-seven passed the exam except for three individuals, and the remaining participants took the exam later and passed. In total, eighty of the pilot's participants took and passed the exam. The City received revenue totaling $26,800 through licensing fees and provided new business opportunities for participants.

As of July 2015—QEDC works with community partners, local elected officials and press to market the program. Training occurs at facilities where community partners are located. The economic impact potential of this program has been tremendous for the city, giving small businesses the opportunity to generate city revenue from licensing and increased sales revenue due to new contracts. Thirty-four cohorts totaling 450 participants have participated. Three hundred and seventy-six trainees have become licensed (76 percent immigrant) and 155 businesses have been started. Approximately $153,000 in city revenue has been generated from licensing fees.

QEDC reports that the keys to the success of the program include (1) promotional support from local officials, (2) working with DCA to learn about procedural changes and provide trainees guidance, (3) hiring instructors for multiple locations with multiple language (English, Spanish, Mandarin) capabilities, and (4) fee-based training that has attracted more committed trainees and facilitated sponsorships.

The HICT program has continued and expanded in size and diversity. Through 2017, 55 cohorts have been trained, totaling 674 people with 505 receiving contractor licenses. Programs have been run in English, Spanish, and Mandarin. This resulted in participants starting 268 businesses (Bornstein, 2017).

Year 2: CAMBA—Mobilize Your Business—Winner

Mobilize Your Business (MYB) is a training program that teaches low- and moderate-income entrepreneurs to use tablet-based technology to transform their cash-and-carry businesses into bankable businesses.

Pilot—During the pilot, seventy-one participants attended training. Approximately 63 percent of participants were existing business owners and 92 percent completed the full three-class series. More than 90 percent were minority business owners in industries that included retail, wholesale and manufacturing. Outcomes of the pilot included:

-   74 percent of business owners implemented at least one of the MYB applications or began using a tablet for business
-   58 percent of business owners began accepting credit cards after taking the class and 83 percent of those who began using Square had increased credit card sales using mobile POS
-   56 percent converted to electronic bookkeeping from a paper-based business
-   48% implemented social media and all of them reported that it helped their business

As of July 2015—In order to track impact, CAMBA followed up with businesses that took the MYB course and learned that implementation of new technology was a major challenge. Although participants were comfortable using the technology in the classroom, they were not successful in its implementation. CAMBA realized that a more labor-intensive process was necessary at the business owner's location to increase technology adoption. CAMBA raised funding from the United States Small Business Administration to hire a full-time technology trainer for a MYB Plus (MYB+) program.

After the small biz owner attends the MYB workshop suite, CAMBA provides one-on-one coaching/assistance regarding technology implementation on site (accepting credit cards, accounting systems, website, and social media marketing). In addition, MYB+ entails an individualized intensive 360 degree assessment of the business and the application of a Value Stream Mapping process (using principles of LEAN) to also identify operational areas of the business in need of improvement and identify and implement free or low-cost solutions, which may or may not be technological in nature.

Over 250 attendees have participated and benefited from MYB, and 80 percent have started accepting credit cards, implemented a mobile accounting system or adopted a social media marketing strategy. Workshop attendees were African American, Caribbean, Hispanic, Asian, and Russian. Seventy-eight businesses applied for the MYB+ and twenty-seven completed the program. Of the twenty-seven who completed the program, six implemented social media, eight implemented POS systems, ten implemented a cloud accounting system, and three built a website.

In 2014 at the Corporation for Enterprise Development Asset Learning Conference, CAMBA, along with nine other finalists, competed in a Shark Tank Small Business Challenge for the best social venture addressing challenges of small business owners, and MYB won the first prize of $10,000 from Master Card.

In 2016 CAMBA received additional funding from the SBA to provide MYB Plus curriculum to worker owner cooperatives in addition to the organization's small business owner constituency. Training was also expanded to Brooklyn, Bronx and Queens. CAMBA expects to expand MYB Plus nationally in 2018 and 2019 and scale their efforts via a "train the trainer" model.

CAMBA reports that the key to success can be attributed to paying greater attention to their clients' needs. As with many service providers, they believed they had the cure for their client's challenges. However, communicating with clients allowed CAMBA to understand better why they were hesitant to formalize themselves, adapt technology or operate differently. Thus, they were able to come up with tailored solutions to their clients' very specific challenges and add a great deal of value (Roldan, 2017).

Year 3: SoBRO—The United Business Cooperative (UBC)—Winner

UBC is a bottom-up approach for collective purchasing power among immigrant hospitality businesses.

In 2013, New York City regulators announced that in 2016 businesses would only be able to use biodegradable materials (use of Styrofoam and plastic would be illegal). Even though this will be good for the environment, this new regulation will raise the cost of paper goods by 20–30 percent. In reaction to this news, a large group of restaurant owners engaged SoBRO's assistance in determining how to handle this situation. SoBRO saw this as an opportunity to protect, enhance and build the skills base of this group of entrepreneurs. During their conversations with these businesses, the idea of a purchasing cooperative that would reduce their costs emerged as a good way to combat the cost of these new regulations. Additionally, their conversations revealed that joint marketing efforts and skills training would also be beneficial to these businesses.

Pilot—SoBRO began formalizing the concept of The United Business Cooperative as a group of immigrant-operated restaurants from the Bronx and Northern Manhattan. Led by SoBRO, UBC is New York City's first group purchasing organization for local restaurants and multi-unit food service operators. The goal of the UBC is for member businesses to maximize profits, reduce costs, and develop best practices to protect the community and economic development in target areas. SoBRO envisioned that they would provide this collective with hands-on technical assistance and hospitality best practices, cost savings for collective purchasing, access to a revolving loan fund created by member dues, and access to reduced costs for fixed costs contractors.

During the pilot SoBRO conducted a needs assessment survey and worked with a group of forty-five prospective UBC members to analyze and prioritize their needs. They also organized the UBC legal framework and incorporated as a legal New York State entity. SoBRO provided 200 hours of one-on-one technical assistance, conducted twenty-five hours of group meetings, provided sixty referrals to technical assistance providers, investigated the implementation of a revolving loan fund, identified a home office space, and began connecting UBC members with food suppliers for enhanced purchasing power. A portion of the technical assistance (Square training) for ten members was conducted via CAMBA's MYB program (see above). Several members received advanced training from an IT professional they hired.

As of June 2015—The UBC is formally registered as an entity with thirty member restaurants and is located in SoBRO's small business incubator. A bank account was established, and three members have gone through an expansion. Seven members completed a collective purchase of nonperishables and paper goods and in June 2015 an additional purchase by ten members was in process. Two members received loans from a loan fund established with prize money from the THRIVE competition.

To prepare for the upcoming regulation of Styrofoam products, SoBRO introduced its membership to Produce Bio Pak, a sustainable packaging manufacturer. SoBRO is currently working with an evaluation team from New York University to assist them with evaluating the success of the cooperative model and its potential replication. Regarding health and local foods integration, SoBRO is having discussions with its members on incorporating healthier menu options. They also conducted a market analysis of local farmers and the local farming industry that revealed that the future direction of the industry is one of growth and specialization.

SoBRO reported that making sure their UBC constituents feel that having a network of support has been very beneficial as well as providing them with additional technical assistance. Nonetheless, the formal cooperative purchasing did not continue past the pilot. SoBro continues to direct businesses to local suppliers that can meet the needs of small businesses (Heyman, 2017).

Observations

The THRIVE model represents a unique approach to fostering economic development in immigrant communities. It is a model that encouraged innovation. As the concept of innovation is often misunderstood, it needed to be explained and reinforced. The concept was stressed and explained more thoroughly in Year 2 marketing materials. Innovation had to be stressed during the TA sessions as well. A weakness inherent to the model however is that larger ESOs have an advantage. Larger organizations have more resources thus enabling them to have more impact. Smaller ESOs may have been more agile and experimental in their proposed approach; however, because scalability and implementation were critical judging criteria, the Competition tended to favor the larger organizations.

Professional management and guidance of ESOs as social entrepreneurial ventures was a necessary factor that contributed to successful outcomes. Technical assistance is necessary. Finalist ESOs had limited business entrepreneurship acumen and business development orientation; therefore, technical assistance was required for the pilot period. Most are accustomed to writing proposals for funding but not for developing new, sustainable, and scalable ideas. It was helpful to encourage finalists to think of themselves as "social entrepreneurs," creating economic and social value, as they approached business plan writing. The finalists needed to take a more strategic approach to launching, implementing and modifying the pilot and its teachings into a comprehensive plan. Finalists were also required to take a data-driven approach to understanding in which direction to pivot.

The business planning process was valuable and effective, and business acumen among finalists noticeably improved by the end of the Competition. Both mentors and finalists observed this. The disciplined thinking required by the process not only improved the plans over the six-month period but enhanced the organizational capability of the finalist ESOs as well.

Marketing planning also helped engender a customer focus. Participating ESOs came to the Competition with a clinical perception of their clients—individuals that they serve through the provision of a set of services. Through the business planning exercise, they came to see their clients as customers for whom they were adding value by fulfilling an expressed need. The ESOs' offerings must meet this need, or their (the ESOs) enterprise will fail. This helped the ESOs to appreciate the pilot project as a test bed of the value-adding propensity of their services.

The requirement of a pilot program was an effective strategy. The pilot program worked well as a lean start-up (Blank & Dorf, 2012) exercise that forced finalists to test their hypotheses with their immigrant entrepreneur clients, prove or disprove them, and adjust before incorporating them into their business plans. The finalists' successes were enhanced by their engagement in their communities. We found that participating ESOs had an in-depth knowledge of the communities they serve. This involvement enabled them to develop innovative programs that blended the familiar with the new, making them more relevant to client immigrant entrepreneurs. Encouraging experimentation with collaboration provided a gateway for finalists to propose projects that are more sophisticated. THRIVE 3 included three collaborative projects, which facilitated a multi-partner approach that incorporated a multi-perspective methodology to addressing problems.

A competition modeling THRIVE can be expensive and labor intensive. Fundraising was required of the NYCEDC to fund Competition prize money. Year 1 prize money totaled $250,000 and Year 2 totaled $350,000, while in Year 3 a total of $225,000 was awarded. Consultant program manager fees were an additional cost as well as the marketing expense. Program managers were required of NYCEDC and Baruch College, as well as a technical assistance team and research interns. Costs (prizes and fees) are relative and can be lowered in different markets.

Competition encouraged organizations to try new things. The competition provided incentive, resources and a vehicle for testing new ideas. This helped to enhance the assistance provided to immigrant entrepreneurs in New York City. To put it another way, competition winners were not the only beneficiaries of the THRIVE competition. All participating ESOs improved their practice and offerings, benefitting all the immigrant entrepreneurs they serve. The benefit was arguably more widespread than merely holding a competition for immigrant entrepreneurs.

It was beneficial to have a government entity collaborate with an educational institution as well as a foundation to offset the costs of the competition. Due to the political nature of local economic development and the fact that participating ESOs are politically connected, a government partner lent credibility and political acumen to the process. Likewise, a public local college with ties to the immigrant community was valuable as well.

ESOs' capability to address the transaction barriers faced by immigrants is enhanced since the Competition helped the finalists deal with transaction barriers more efficiently and effectively. As noted earlier, through its innovative program, the Queens Economic Development Corporation was successful in getting New York City to offer its contractor's licensing exam in other languages. In addition, SoBRO's United Business Cooperative initiative provided restaurant owners with assistance in identifying a suitable, sustainable packaging manufacturer.

All of this suggests that a business plan competition can be an effective way to address many of the shortcomings of ESOs noted earlier. More specifically, the market analysis component of business planning taught these organizations to understand better the true needs of their client entrepreneurs and how to tailor their services to those needs, as opposed to forcing the entrepreneurs to mold their needs to the services offered. That is, the ESOs became customer focused. Similarly, the ESOs became entrepreneur developers, not merely service providers. After coming into the Competition perceiving innovation as being only the generation of a new idea, they learned that it is not innovation until the new service is successfully delivered to customers (clients) in a high quality, repeatable, scalable, and sustainable way. The six-month pilot/planning process drove the innovation concept home. There is no question that entrepreneurship and business acumen were increased among Competition finalists. Finally, one of the most vexing concepts posed to these nonprofits was that of scaling, or growth. The Competition taught them that, for ESOs, scaling is about maximizing their mission's reach—developing more immigrant entrepreneurs. This is something that does not happen naturally but must be carefully planned and executed.

The Economic Development Corporation did not continue to run Project THRIVE, but the Department of Small Business Services initiated a program with $500,000 in annual prizes awarded to partnerships formed between nonprofits and tech companies that developed solutions to problems on the administration's agenda such as parking, sanitation, or affordable housing (Small Business Services, 2017).

Conclusion

Encouraging immigrant entrepreneurship as a community economic development strategy has much potential. To be effective, however, communities need to be aware of the current quality of their ESOs and be willing to invest in improving them. One approach is to stage a business plan competition to encourage innovation and improved efficiency and effectiveness among ESOs. Competition THRIVE in New York City provides a potential model for successfully accomplishing this.

It should be acknowledged, however, that this is only one case in one location. The economy and population density of New York City are clearly idiosyncratic, as is its concentration of immigrants. However, with modification for the local context, this competition has basic elements that could be applied anywhere, not the least of which is the collaboration of government, business, and institutions of higher education that brings resources and expertise to an entrepreneurship-focused community economic development effort.

The case of Competition THRIVE tends to bear out the benefits of business plan competitions to entrepreneurs and entrepreneurship identified in the literature. Participating ESOs did develop management, operational, marketing, and other business skills that they did not necessarily have before the competition. Competitors learned the value of collaboration and teamwork and the power in building networks beyond the normal scope of their work. They also demonstrated an ability to integrate the various elements of business in their pilots and their business plans. The incentive of prize money and access to mentors kept them focused and committed to the enterprise. Ultimately, they improved their practice in demonstrable ways.

Competition THRIVE represents an innovative approach to mitigating wealth inequality. It supports the work of the social entrepreneurs who, in turn, support entrepreneurship by lower-income immigrant commercial entrepreneurs. This facilitates wealth building and increases the economic mobility of these entrepreneurs.

References

Aldrich, H.E., & Martinez, M.A. (2001). Many are called, but few are chosen: An evolutionary perspective for the study of entrepreneurship. *Entrepreneurship Theory and Practice* 25 (4): 41–56.

Blank, S., & Dorf, B. (2012). *The startup owner's manual: The step-by-step guide to building a great company*. Pescadero, CA: K&S Ranch.

Bluestein, A. (2017). The most entrepreneurial group in America wasn't born in America. *Inc. com*. May 4, 2017.

Bornstein, S. (2017). Telephone interview with Seth Bornstein, conducted September 5, 2017.

Boter, H., & Lundstrom, A. (2005). SME perspectives on business support services: The role of company size, industry and location. *Journal of Small Business and Enterprise Development* 12 (2): 244–258.

Bowles, J., & Colton, T. (2007). *A world of opportunity*. New York: Center for an Urban Future.

Brinckmann, J., Grichnik, D., & Kapsa, D. (2009). Should entrepreneurs plan or just storm the castle? A meta-analysis on contextual factors impacting the business planning-performance relationship in small firms. *Journal of Business Venturing* 25 (1): 24–40.

Byrne, F. (2002). Pay-offs from pursuit of glittering prizes. *Financial Times* 12 (September): 14.

Calman, L., Brunton, L., & Molassiotis, A. (2013). Developing longitudinal qualitative designs: Lessons learned and recommendations for health services research. *BMC Medical Research Methodology* 13: 14–24.

Chao-Tung, W., & Yi Wen, C. (2007). The innovation process of entrepreneurial teams in dynamic business plan competitions: From the sense-making perspective. *International Journal of Technology Management* 39 (3/4): 346.

Creswell, J. (1998). *Research design: Qualitative, quantitative, and mixed methods approaches* (2nd Ed.). Thousand Oaks, CA: Sage.

Curran, J. (2000). What is small business policy in the UK for? Evaluation and assessing small business policies. *International Small Business Journal* 18 (3): 36–50.

De Faoite, D., Henry, C., Johnston, K., & van der Sijde, P. (2003). Entrepreneurs' attitudes to training and support initiatives: Evidence from Ireland and The Netherlands. *Journal of Small Business and Enterprise Development* 11 (4): 440–448.

Durr, M., Lyons, T.S., & Lichtenstein, G.A. (2000). Identifying the unique needs of urban entrepreneurs: African American skill set development. *Race and Society* 3 (1): 75–90.

Funkhouser, M. (2012). A competition for ideas in public policy. *Governing*, March 29. Accessed on November 14, 2016. Retrieved from http://www.governing.com/col-public-policy-challenge-fels-university-pennsylvania-governing-institute.html.

Gu, Q., Karoly, L.A., & Zissimopoulos, J.M. (2008). Small business assistance programs in the United States: An analysis of what they are, how well they perform, and how we can learn more about them, *RAND Working Paper No. WR-603-EMKF*. Retrieved from https://papers.ssm.com/sol3/papers.cfm?abstract_id=1295625. Accessed August 29, 2017.

Hallam, C., de la Vina, L., Leffel, A., & Agrawal, M. (2014). Accelerating collegiate entrepreneurship (ACE): The architecture of a university entrepreneurial ecosystem encompassing an intercollegiate venture experience. *Journal of Business and Entrepreneurship* 26 (2): 95–116.

Hart, D.M., & Acs, Z.J. (2011). High-tech immigrant entrepreneurship in the United States. *Economic Development Quarterly* 25 (2): 16–29.

Henry, C., Hill, F., & Leitch, C. (2003). Developing a coherent enterprise support policy: A new challenge for governments. *Environment and Planning C: Government and Policy* 21: 3–19.

Heyman, A. (2017). Telephone interview with A. Heyman, conducted September 29, 2017.

Heriot, K.C., Dickes, L., & Jauregui, A. (2017). Boots2Business: An early view of an SBA outreach program. *Small Business Institute Journal* 13 (1): 1–15.

Hurst, B. (2000). Reaping rewards not just from winning, but from taking part. *Financial Times* 23 (November): 18.

Jones, A., & Jones, P. (2011). 'Making an impact': A profile of a business planning competition in a university. *Education & Training* 53 (8/9): 704–721.

Jackson, C. (2015). Lessons from the Kauffman Index: Immigrants are infused with entrepreneurial energy. Retrieved from http://kauffman.org/blogs/growthology/2015/06lessons-from-the-kauffman-index-immigrants. Accessed August 30, 2017.

Kayne, J.A. (2002). Promoting and supporting an entrepreneurship-based economy in Maine. *Augusta, ME: Ewing Marion Kauffman Foundation and Entrepreneurial Working Group/ Maine Small Business Commission.*

Kickul, J., & Lyons, T.S. (2016). *Understanding social entrepreneurship: The relentless pursuit of mission in an ever changing world* (2nd Ed.). New York: Routledge.

Lange, J.E., Mollov, A., Pearlmutter, M., Singh, S., & Bygrave. W.D. (2007). Pre-start-up formal business plans and post-start-up performance: A study of 116 new ventures. *Venture Capital* 9 (4): 237–256.

Lichtenstein, G.A., & Lyons, T.S. (2010). Investing in entrepreneurs: A strategic approach for strengthening your regional and community economy. Santa Barbara, CA: Praeger/ ABC-CLIO.

Lichtenstein, G.A., & Lyons, T.S. (2001). The entrepreneurial development system: Transforming business talent and community economies. *Economic Development Quarterly* 15 (1): 3–20.

Lichtenstein, G. A., & Lyons, T.S. (1996). *Incubating new enterprises: A guide to successful practice.* Washington, DC: The Aspen Institute.

Lichtenstein, G.A., Lyons, T.S., & Kutzhanova, N. (2004). Building entrepreneurial communities: The appropriate role of enterprise development activities. *Journal of the Community Development Society* 35 (1): 5–24.

Liu, C.Y. (2012). Intrametropolitan opportunity structure and the self-employment of Asian and Latino immigrants. *Economic Development Quarterly* 26 (2): 178–192.

McKenzie, D. (2015). Identifying and spurring high-growth entrepreneurship: Experimental evidence from a business plan competition. *World Bank Policy Working Paper No. 7391.*

New American Economy (2016). Reason for reform: entrepreneurship. Retrieved from http:// www.newamericaneconomy.org/wp-content/uploads/2016/12/Entrepreneur.pdf. Accessed August 30, 2017.

New York City, Department of Small Business Services, Accessed on September 29, 2017 (http:// www1.nyc.gov/site/sbs/neighborhoods/neighborhood-challenge.page).

Podsakoff, P.M., & Organ, D.W. (1986). Self-reports in organizational research: Problems and prospects. *Journal of Management* 12 (4): 531–544.

Roldan, I. (2017). Telephone interview with I. Roldan, September 29, 2017.

Russell, R., Atchison, M., & Brooks, R. (2008). Business plan competitions in tertiary institutions: Encouraging entrepreneurship education. *Journal of Higher Education Policy and Management* 30 (2): 123–138.

Schwartz, M., Goethner, M., Michelson, C., & Waldmann, N. (2013). Start-up competitions as an instrument of entrepreneurial policy: The German experience. *European Planning Studies* 21 (10): 1578–1597.

Shane, S., & Delmar, F. (2004). Planning for the market: Business planning before marketing and the continuation of organizing efforts. *Journal of Business Venturing* 19: 767–785.

Shinnar, R.S., Aguilera, M.B., & Lyons, T.S. (2011). Co-ethnic markets: Financial penalty or opportunity. *International Business Review* 20 (6): 646–658.

Stake, R.E. (1995). *The art of case study research.* Thousand Oaks, CA: Sage.

Streb, C.K. (2010). Exploratory case study. In A.J. Mills, G. Durepos, & E. Wiebe, *Encyclopedia of Case Study Research* (pp. 373–374). Thousand Oaks, CA: Sage.

Sullivan, R. (2000). Entrepreneurial learning and mentoring. *International Journal of Entrepreneurial Behavior and Research* 6: 160–175.

Thomas, D.F., Gudmundson, D., Turner, K., & Suhr, D. (2014). Business plan competitions and their impact on new ventures' business models. *Journal of Strategic Innovation and Sustainability* 10 (1): 34--48.

Tienda, M., & Raijman, R. (2004). Promoting Hispanic immigrant entrepreneurship in Chicago. *Journal of Developmental Entrepreneurship* 9 (1): 1–22.

U. S. Census Bureau. (2012). American *Community Survey*, 1-Year Sample.

Watson, K., McGowan, P., & Smith, P. (2015). Leveraging effectual means through business plan competition participation. *Industry & Higher Education* 29 (6): 481–492.

Yin, R.K. (2003). *Case study research: Design and methods* (3rd Ed.). Thousand Oaks, CA: Sage.

Zimmerman, J. (2012). Using business plans for teaching entrepreneurship. *American Journal of Business Education (On-line):* 5 (6).

Chapter 6
An Example from Chicago: The West Side Business Xcelerator

Arguably, social entrepreneurship strategies that address wealth inequality have achieved impressive results around the world in a number of different contexts, as demonstrated throughout this book. However, it is sometimes assumed that, while social enterprise may be a good idea for tribal societies or developing countries, it is not a viable solution for the economy and culture of the United States. This is often the case in low-income, minority communities in America, where investors and traditional entrepreneurial support organizations are reluctant to assist local ventures because they perceive that the social entrepreneurship model is not suited for them; and therefore, they will not be successful.

The underlying premise of social entrepreneurship is that support must be provided in ways beyond simply the economic because economic success is built on a firm foundation of prosperity in other aspects of the community. Ignoring this can create a vicious cycle where failure caused by lack of appropriate support is used to justify not investing in such support in the future. This dilemma will be explored through the lens of Chicago's West Side Xcelerator and West Side Forward programs operated by a nongovernmental organization called Bethel New Life.

History of Chicago's West Side

This book as a whole is a testament to the growing concerns about wealth inequality since the 1960s and 1970s in all regions of the country and around the world. However, Chicago has become something of a poster child for these trends, as it represents a particularly sharp division between the haves and the have-nots, often along racial lines. According to data collected in 2014, Chicago is 72 percent segregated (representing the percentage of residents who would have to move to desegregate the area), compared to other major cities, like New York, which have a segregation percentage in the low- to mid-sixties. This data also shows that blacks in Chicago have more than doubled both the poverty and the employment rate of whites as well as the ever increasing wage gap, with the wealthy experiencing a 33 percent income increase between 1990 and 2012, while the poor experienced a 4 percent decrease during the same period (Luhby, 2016).

DOI 10.1515/9781547400461-006

Far West Side

See and Do
1. Aguijón Theater
2. Apollos 2000
3. Garfield Park Conservatory
4. Laramie State Bank Building
5. Sears Tower
6. Walser House

Buy
1. Brickyard Mall
2. Markski's CDs
3. Out of the Past Records

Eat
1. Cafe Colao
2. Feed
3. Grota's
4. Home Run Inn Pizzeria
5. La Bruquena
6. La Palma
7. Los Dos Laredos
8. Lou Malnati's
9. MacArthur's
10. Maiz
11. Mi Tierra
12. Operetta
13. Peeples Taco Place
14. Taquerías Atotonilco

16. Taquería Los Comales
17. Wallace's Catfish Corner

Drink
1. California Clipper
2. The Continental
3. Jedynka Club
4. La Justicia
5. Los Globos
6. Rooster Palace

Sleep
1. Fullerton Hotel
2. Grand Motel West
3. Hotel Norford
4. North Hotel

Contact
1. Austin Library
2. Douglass Library
3. Galewood-Montclare Library
4. Humboldt Park Library
5. Legler Branch
6. Marshall Square Library
7. North Austin Library
8. North Pulaski Library
9. Portage-Cragin Library
10. Toman Library
11. West Belmont Library
12. West Chicago Ave Library

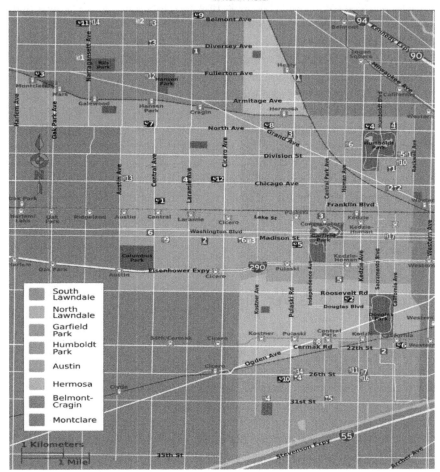

Source: Fitzgerald, P. (2007). Chicago's far West Side district, street map. Map [online]. Retrieved from https://en.wikivoyage.org/wiki/Chicago/Far_West_Side#/media/File:Far_West_Side_map.png. Accessed July 26, 2018.

Figure 6.1: The neighborhoods of Chicago's West Side

Chicago's West Side (see Figure 6.1) became a part of these trends in the early to mid 1900s during the great migration, when it received a large influx of southern emigres, fleeing poverty and racial discrimination, leading the area to become known as the "plantation wards." However, these newcomers were hampered in their ability to improve their situation due to the area being strictly controlled by wealthy white political bosses and the mob who used intimidation and violence to maintain the racial and economic status quo, as can be seen in the case of Benjamin Lewis. He became the only Chicago alderman murdered in office after West Side residents succeeded in electing him against the will of the mob and bosses in 1963, part of a trend that led to the explosion of rioting in the area in 1968 after the Martin Luther King assassination (Moser, 2018).

In the time since then, the West Side has experienced pressures such as the closing of factories that have affected the working class all across the country. However, the West Side also includes a collection of features that make this process particularly devastating for the economy and quality of life in the area. These includes policies like redlining, that has a long history of preventing poor and minority individuals from purchasing homes in the area, which has caused them to instead be funneled into government housing projects (Semuels, 2018), as well as transit issues that restrict mobility. Because the transit system in Chicago is arranged like the spokes of a wheel radiating from downtown, and is primarily focused on the north-south corridor along the lakeshore, large sections of the city have poor transit coverage. This, combined with the fact that poor people may not be able to afford cars, means that as employment opportunities are increasingly concentrated in the downtown area and the suburbs, many residents of the West Side are rendered incapable of accessing those opportunities (Semuels, 2018).

This lack of opportunities creates a vicious cycle, where West Side residents are unable to get jobs and, therefore, lack income to reinvest in their community, leading to more businesses moving away and further decreases in quality of life. Add to this a lack of positive role models and inspirations for young people in the community. A decrease in wealth and property values also means a decrease in funding for education, which also means a decrease in life skills and resume support, compounding the employment problems (Semuels, 2018). These factors combine to cause an increase in crime in the area to such an extent that the West Side has become a key factor in the city of Chicago being labeled as America's "murder capitol." Although statistics indicate that murders in Chicago have been on the decrease for many years, dropping 20 percent in 2013 alone, the West Side has actually experienced an increase in crime, with a murder rate as much as eighty times that of areas on the north and east sides of the city (Young, 2014). This further exacerbates the image of the West Side as an undesirable area. Because of the crime rate, residents may be reluctant to move there, businesses may be unwilling to locate there, and some in other areas of the city may even be hesitant to hire residents of the area (Semules, 2018). All of these factors work together to create the economic situation on the West Side, which calls for interventions like the West Side Xcelerator.

The West Side Xcelerator

The West Side Xcelerator was an unsuccessful experiment by Bethel New Life to help entrepreneurs in this largely low-income, minority community to create wealth by growing their businesses. This was to be accomplished by connecting them with markets outside the community (Bethel New Life, 2016). In this way, it was acting as a true accelerator, seeking to engage its client entrepreneurs directly with markets and, in so doing, speeding up the growth of their companies (Sepulveda, 2012). This approach was an attempt to address the fact that minority entrepreneurs tend to sell within their own neighborhoods to customers of the same ethnicity. Research has shown that this strategy carries a financial penalty to these entrepreneurs (Shinnar et al., 2011). However, if minority businesses pursue a strategy of market expansion, they must be prepared to meet the demands of these larger markets. It can not be assumed that merely connecting them to these markets is sufficient. For this reason, the accelerator also sought to improve the skills of its client entrepreneurs.

The West Side Xcelerator focused its efforts on supporting entrepreneurs whose businesses had passed the start-up phase but were not yet in the true growth stage. These companies are not yet perceived as being qualified for venture capital or other forms of equity investment. The existing traditional entrepreneurship support organizations did not have the capacity or capability to help them become investment ready; so, these entrepreneurs found themselves in a state of limbo. The accelerator was designed to fill this void by working with entrepreneurs from the West Side whose companies had the necessary business goals that would allow them to generate $500,000–$3 million in revenue and engage 5–25 employees (Bethel New Life, 2016), commonly referred to as Stage 2 businesses.

The support to these entrepreneurs attempted to be comprehensive. Through training and coaching, the accelerator sought to develop their entrepreneurship skills. Specifically, assistance with market research, operations management, and strategic planning was offered. The accelerator also established the West Side Investment Fund as a source of growth capital for their client companies (Bethel New Life, 2016).

While the West Side Xcelerator ultimately did not succeed, in the spirit of entrepreneurship, it should not be perceived as a failure. The lessons learned can be used to inform future efforts to build wealth through entrepreneurship, particularly in low-income urban contexts.

The Barriers to Success

In order to understand more fully the issues and challenges facing this program, it is necessary to take a step back and examine the challenges, historical and current, that have faced attempts at urban economic development and entrepreneurship. A useful resource on this particular topic is an article published in the journal *Race & Society* entitled "Identifying the Unique Needs of Urban Entrepreneurs: African American Skill Set Development" by Marlese Durr, Thomas S. Lyons, and Gregg A. Lichtenstein, which provides an in-depth historical trajectory of economic hurdles faced by inner city and minority groups. This article points out that, historically, "African Americans, many of whom lacked educational experiences associated with economic and enterprise development were excluded from being considered as potential investors/partners in community-wide efforts to encourage and sustain economic development" (Durr et al., 2000: 76). Durr, Lyons, and Lichtenstein go on to say that "The massive disinvestment in the city's urban core has left that part of the metropolitan region a wasteland (e.g., dilapidated business storefronts, ghost-like business areas with high rates of unemployment, deteriorating housing stock, high rates of crime, and staggering social problems). The inner-cities became a location in which few if any investors with capital sought to launch new enterprises because the people who live in these areas are those who literally cannot afford to escape, and are typically members of minority groups" (Durr et al., 2000: 76).

Further, the article points out that, even as historical factors like overt racism have waned in some areas, other factors have continued to operate, or have even grown in their severity, that continue to keep urban communities trapped in poverty. "Unlike the historical past, where racial discrimination played a major role in business investment and development for African Americans, contemporary constraints to investment within these communities are grounded in economic shifts over the past three decades, which reduced employment opportunities, limiting expansion, or elimination, of their employment bases or decreasing their revenue bases. In tandem with these structural changes, African Americans receive limited opportunities for entrepreneurial mentoring to shore up skills and experiences associated with operating a business" (Durr et al., 2000: 77). These passages encapsulate the dual pronged dilemma involving inner city economies.

The issues the article describes, such as high crime rates and poor housing, are common problems caused by poverty, and the strategy for eliminating them is to strengthen the community as a whole. However, poverty has also stripped these individuals of the skills needed to make the needed economic improvements; and thus, investors avoid the inner city as a poor investment for the very reasons their support is so badly needed. This lack of investment means that inner city residents receive neither the material nor educational resources needed to improve their lot, resources the investors readily supply to entrepreneurial projects elsewhere. This means that the problems will persist, and the urban environment will continue to be seen as a bad investment.

Citing Porter (1995), the article also points out that urban environments have certain advantages that otherwise would make them attractive investment opportunities, pointing out that they are "places where residents possess a natural advantage for economic development because of their central location, local market demand, integration of regional clusters, and building costs. He maintains that these assets encourage the growth and formation of companies, which can exploit these advantages, and take root in the inner-city. Nevertheless, this model does not necessarily place African Americans within the calculus of small business development or expansion. As a potential solution to this problem, many such communities have begun to engage in enterprise development" (Durr et al., 2000: 76). In addition to the advantages described above, there is also a desire for urban development to reduce poverty and its attendant issues, such as crime. However, the authors argue that the current approaches to doing this have significant flaws in their methods (Durr et al., 2000: 77–78):

> National, state, and local governments have attempted numerous interventions over the years in an effort to revitalize the economies of U.S. urban cores, with only limited success. Those interventions have tended to follow one of two strategies. The first is an effort to attract outside investment. This has generally focused on initiatives to encourage major corporations to locate facilities in the urban core to create jobs for local residents and provide needed services. Examples of this strategy are many and include programs to bring major chain supermarkets into the inner-city or to provide financial incentives to encourage manufactures to build new plants in these communities. Critics of these programs point out that they tend to "colonize" urban communities by using their low-wage workforce to generate profits that are exported to the corporation in question's home offices.

This shows both the desire to improve inner city economies and the lack of an effective strategy for doing so. It also raises the important concern that improving the surface economy of an area is not the same thing as meeting the needs of the residents of that area. When outside businesses move in to an urban community and then profits are exported elsewhere, the net economic effect on the community, itself, will be minimal. This is the opposite of the social entrepreneurship approach where, as much as is possible, resources are invested by the community and resources produced are reinvested back into the community.

Some investors have become aware of this and are making a shift toward more community focused entrepreneurship endeavors, with New Bethel's West Side Xcelerator in Chicago being one of these programs. As Durr et al. explain, "The second general urban economic development strategy has been an attempt to foster local, community-based economic activity and investment. Its focus is on enterprise development, as opposed to business attraction. This strategy includes a host of programs that are presently in good currency, among them enterprise and empowerment zones, empowerment business incubation programs, micro-lending programs, community banking, cooperatives, minority business development centers, etc." (Durr et al., 2000: 78). This approach provides a structure compatible with social entrepreneurship, which could be used to build a firm foundation for community development. The fact that these authors go on to raise concerns about the efficacy of such programs as well as whether or not they are being managed properly shows that, in their current state, they are far from a miracle cure, especially in the inner city.

Issues with efficacy and management (whether or not the right approach was taken) have certainly played a role in the history of the West Side Xcelerator. As its name indicates, the organization chose to operate as an accelerator rather than using the older model of a business incubator. The white paper "Bethel Business Accelerator West Side Chicago Business Sector White Paper" by Marvin Austin, Robert Harris, and Edward Coleman (2014), as part of its goal of determining the feasibility and best practices of the West Side Accelerator venture, places emphasis on the key distinctions between the two. The decision to go with an accelerator model rather than an incubator makes a certain amount of sense, given the criticism of incubators by Durr, Lyons, and Lichtenstein. "The basic problem with these approaches is that they are treated as 'generic' programs designed to fit any enterprise development situation. The focus is on structure, or form, as opposed to the function of the program. For example, in business incubation the objective is to create the most effective incubator: one, it is assumed, that will be successful in all contexts and under all circumstances. Thus, the focus is on the optimal size of the incubator facility, the appropriate number and type of client entrepreneurs, the most desirable mix of pre-packaged service offerings, etc. It is believed that this model incubator can then be superimposed on any landscape with positive results; yet, the fact remains that incubation programs in the U.S. are closing their doors at a rate of one per month" (Durr et al., 2000: 78). However, it is not clear that an accelerator would be any less vulnerable to these concerns.

According to Austin and colleagues, "The Seed Accelerator derives much of its characteristics from the business incubator; their services often include pre-seed investments (usually in exchange for equity) and the focus is on business model innovation. In contrast to an incubator, the seed accelerator views the startup period as short, and startups are often supported in cohort batches or 'classes' during a seed acceleration program. But, accelerators are not considered 'protected' nurturing environments, like the business incubator. The best method to measure MBA organizations is by their community actions and affiliations: jobs creation, years in service, corporate partnerships and entrepreneurial results" (Austin et al., 2014: 42). In this description, the focus is on the form rather than the function of the accelerator and the approach described above certainly is not immune to attempts to find an "ideal" one-size-fits-all, accelerator model. In addition, the white paper presents a potentially negative view of accelerators by saying "Essentially, the function of an accelerator is to turn the art of starting a company into a program that can be repeated, churning out valuable companies as if on an assembly line" (Austin et al., 2014: 41). This statement certainly raises suspicions of a formulaic, one-size-fits-all model.

This becomes even more troublesome when taking into account Durr and her colleagues' statement that the function of enterprise development programs is "helping entrepreneurs to overcome the obstacles they face to obtaining the resources necessary to successfully launch and sustain their new businesses" (Durr et al., 2000: 78). "The needs of entrepreneurs are largely determined by the context in which the entrepreneur operates" (Durr et al., 2000: 76). These authors go on to say that "An entrepreneur who operates in an urban context in the United States faces obstacles that are unique to that environment and that individual. These obstacles stem from the conditions of poverty, isolation, racism, and crime, among others that exist there. Any enterprise development program that is used in the urban context must employ practices that are specifically designed to mitigate these obstacles" (Durr et al., 2000: 78). So the question to be asked in order to determine whether an accelerator meets the definition of successful entrepreneurship support in this case is, "Is it is able to meet the specific needs of urban entrepreneurs?"

The fact that Austin et al. describe accelerators as formulaic—"assembly line" style—and of short duration, even rushed, does not make them sound like prime candidates for many entrepreneurial support situations. In light of the unique challenges of the urban environment, the brief time period of support and non-nurturing climate of an accelerator as opposed to an incubator seems particularly worrisome. In addition, Austin et al. argue that the main downsides of accelerators include "the tendency to build small companies, companies can fail after leaving the accelerator, the tendency to attract businesses in trouble, and startups can come to rely too much on them" (Austin et al., 2014: 41) which also is worrisome, given the challenges of the inner city economy. To evaluate more closely the feasibility of the accelerator model, it is necessary to look at these specific challenges in more detail as well the particulars of the West Side Xcelerator's interactions with those challenges.

Durr and colleagues identify four major resources needed for any success-ful entrepreneurial venture: "(1) a business concept; (2) physical resources; (3) core competencies and skills; and (4) market(s)" (Durr et al., 2000: 79). They also classify entrepreneurial challenges into two categories, resource accessibility obstacles and entrepreneurial capacity obstacles, where "Resource accessibility obstacles are those that impact resource supply, while entrepreneurial capac-ity obstacles affect the entrepreneur's own ability to acquire and use required resources" (Durr et al., 2000: 79–80). Each category is further subdivided into more specific categories, with resource accessibility obstacles being divided into availability, visibility, affordability, and transaction barriers (Durr et al., 2000: 80), while entrepreneurial capacity obstacles may be "due to problems with the entrepreneur's own individual self-awareness, accountability, emotional coping ability, skill, and creativity. These obstacles, without question, are the least understood and most ignored by enterprise development programs. They are psy-chological and developmental in nature, and they represent the true complexity of entrepreneurship. Millions of dollars have been spent over the years on enter-prise development activities, and yet failure rates among new businesses remain high. At least part of the explanation for this situation may lie in the fact that the vast majority of enterprise development resources have been targeted at the resource availability obstacles to entrepreneurship at the expense of the entrepre-neurial capacity obstacles" (Durr et al., 2000: 81).

The lack of support for entrepreneurial capacity obstacles seems problematic in general but especially so in low-income inner city environments where, as Durr et al. point out, there is often a lack of entrepreneurial role models and mentor figures that can make them especially vulnerable to entrepreneurial capacity obstacles (Durr et al., 2000: 86). In addition, the fact that many people in this environment engage in entrepreneurship out of need, rather than by choice, may contribute to this deficiency as well: "The limited skills of many inner-city minority employees make them vulnerable to cyclical fluctuations in hiring and to the down-sizing that has characterized the globalization of the economy. They are often the 'last hired and first fired', as one incubation program manager put it. Many find that their only option is to start a business; however, they're not necessarily equipped to do so, nor are they necessarily so inclined" (Durr et al., 2000: 87).

However, the difficulty is not simply the prevalence of entrepreneurial capacity obstacles or a program's general lack of capacity for addressing them. On a larger scale, the issue involves the sheer size and scope of obstacles facing inner city entrepreneurs. Marvin Austin, Senior Director of Economic Development Strategy at the West Side Xcelerator, points out that this population needs support in *all* aspects of entrepreneurship; thus, even if a program was able to provide strong entrepreneurial capacity support, this does not mean that it would be able to provide assistance with all the various aspects of entrepreneurship (Austin, 2017). To make issues more complicated, these various aspects overlap and interconnect, making finding an insertion point for support even more difficult. For example, Durr et al. describe the issues caused by a lack of capital, "the most frequently cited obstacles to minority entrepreneurship in inner-city communities. While responding incubation program managers acknowledged that this is a barrier faced by most entrepreneurs, regardless of race or gender, it is especially acute for minority entrepreneurs. Banks are highly reluctant to make loans to this latter group. Chief among the reasons given for turning down minority business loan applicants are lack of collateral and a bad credit history. Furthermore, inner-city entrepreneurs tend to lack sufficient personal savings, family backing, or friends who are capable of helping them financially—all of which are resources commonly used by majority entrepreneurs" (Durr et al., 2000: 83). These authors go on to explain how the several elements of this particular issue create a complex web that spans a large portion of the entrepreneurial challenges outlined earlier (Durr et al., 2000: 83):

> Obviously, the required resource in question in this scenario is a physical resource: money or capital. Initially, the principal obstacle would appear to be a lack of availability: for urban minority entrepreneur's capital is non-existent or not available in sufficient quantity. However, this may actually involve an affordability barrier: the capital is unaffordable due to collateral requirements or interest charges. A transaction barrier may be involved as well: the entrepreneur lacks the credit history to get access to the capital, even if he/she has the collateral and can pay the interest. Furthermore, the entrepreneur could be facing a capability barrier in that he/she may not know where to get help with a money problem. Finally, the real problem could be a creative obstacle. The urban entrepreneur may lack the entrepreneurial ability to reframe the problem and create a non-traditional solution to the problem of insufficient capital.

This shows how even a single issue can span multiple aspects of an entrepreneurial challenge, requiring the support program to provide assistance across the full spectrum of challenges. If, as Marvin Austin describes, the inner city poor have difficulty obtaining each of the needed resources and skills, this means that the level of comprehensiveness necessary for such a program to be successful could be staggering.

It may now be illustrative to look at the way some of these entrepreneurial challenges relate to experiences at the West Side Xcelerator. Durr et al. point out that "The second most frequently identified obstacle to entrepreneurship in the inner-city was the fact that would-be entrepreneurs are highly deficient in the business and technical skills necessary for innovation, business formation, and business development over the long term...While the list of needed skills...covers a wide variety of competencies, a lack of skills in decision making, business planning and general business acumen were featured" (Durr et al., 2000: 84).

This relates to the West Side Xcelerator in a number of ways, but the most noteworthy is Austin's observation that potential entrepreneurs who passed through the accelerator frequently lacked a strong understanding of market needs or the ability to identify market gaps where demands for goods and services were not being met. In addition, accelerator clients tended to not be ambitious or imaginative in the types of businesses they attempted to start, usually turning to "tried and true" enterprises such as beauty salons, small food services, cleaning services and auto repair shops, which tend to have oversaturated markets and lack growth potential. This may also relate back to the statement above about how many inner city residents become entrepreneurs out of need, not choice; so, not only do they lack an understanding of market demand, but they also select an opportunity with an eye to making some short-term revenue, instead of taking into account its long-term growth potential (Austin, 2017).

Durr et al. also note, "Because inner-city minority entrepreneurs are often low-income and are many times caught up in the social problems that are common to their communities they are inclined to have more personal problems than do other entrepreneurs. This tends to interfere with their ability to successfully start and sustain a business. These problems may range from poor health to single parents with the need for childcare assistance" (Durr et al., 2000: 85). Marvin Austin recognized similar challenges with Westside Xcelerator clients. For example, because operations are so small scale for the reasons described above, in addition to generating the product idea and running the business, the entrepreneur is usually doing all the labor of the business as well and using personally owned, rather than professional, equipment. If the entrepreneur becomes ill, or the personal vehicle they are using for business transportation breaks down, it causes a complete stoppage of business operations (Austin, 2017).

Other challenges are interpersonal in nature. For example, "Minority entrepreneurs have difficulty finding markets for their goods or services, especially outside of their own communities. In some cases, they do not have the necessary contacts. In most cases, however, it is difficult for them to become suppliers to majority-owned corporations because they are often not taken seriously as business people" (Durr et al., 2000: 84–85). According to Austin, a lack of understanding of how the entrepreneurial process works combined with the mistrust inner city residents often feel toward those outside their community renders this barrier even more daunting. While it is true that it is difficult for inner city entrepreneurs to gain outside recognition, in the rare cases where it does happen, further difficulties are encountered because of reluctance on the part of the entrepreneur. He recalls an experience where one of the accelerator clients had developed a product that addressed a true market need and received an offer from an outside distributor, which the client turned down out of fear of being taken advantage of. Austin says the offer was fair and reasonable, but that lack of trust and an understanding of the business system make it hard for inner city entrepreneurs to recognize such opportunities when they see them. The fact that they often do not see them at all likely does not help (Austin, 2016).

Finally, "The relative isolation from the rest of the metropolitan area in which inner-city minority residents tend to live is said to act as a barrier to entrepreneurship as well. This condition serves to make it more difficult to stay abreast of new developments, access resources, and develop markets, among other things. The isolation scenario embodies business concept, physical, core competencies/skills, and market resources. Isolation can yield a lack of visibility and capability regarding new ideas, technologies, sources of information, etc. It can also make resources less available and less affordable. Finally, isolation, itself, is a transaction barrier to the acquisition of resources" (Durr et al., 2000: 87). This isolation contributes to many challenges faced by inner city entrepreneurs, including the lack of familiarity with and understanding of standard business practices described above. Austin explains that the lack of business opportunities on the west side of Chicago is not the issue but rather that these opportunities are not being captured by local residents. Entrepreneurs from other parts of the city come in to the community and fill these market openings. They also hire employees from outside the area, not only denying the locals the chance of income and economic growth but also of the experience that would make them better job candidates or more capable of starting their own businesses in the future (Austin, 2016).

Finally, there is the issue noted previously that, even if an individual is fully competent in all entrepreneurial skills, they might still face difficulty when attempting to operate in an environment that is not conducive to entrepreneurship. This is where the ideal of social entrepreneurship comes in—the understanding that the success or failure of a venture is not solely dependent on the individual or company launching it, but also is impacted by a host of interconnected factors in the context. According to Marvin Austin, two such factors at play on the west side of Chicago involve the reluctance of investors and support programs to provide sufficient resources, and the fact that nonlocal entrepreneurs who start businesses in the area tend to hire nonlocals as employees, as observed above.

Because of the various challenges described here, Bethel New Life scaled back from operating a full-fledged accelerator and is focusing on training programs meant primarily to address the lack of technical skills and the corresponding lack of innovation in addressing market needs, with a focus on things like computer skills and 3D printing (Austin, 2016). While such programs, doubtless, have the potential to do much good, they are a long way from the scale of social enterprise required to lift the West Side community. However, Bethel New Life has a plan to address this.

In addition to their efforts surrounding the West Side Accelerator, Bethel New Life is also involved in the West Side Forward project, a plan to significantly reduce poverty on the west side of Chicago. The plan for this project displays the sheer scope necessary to make an actual change in the poverty level. This would require the creation of 36,000 jobs on the west side, filling those jobs with west side residents and then finding employment elsewhere in Chicago for a further 51,000 west side residents, for a total of 87,000 new earners from the community. Further, it would be necessary to provide support services to ensure job retention for these new earners at a level of 75 percent after one year and a retention rate of 85 percent at the end of the second year of those retained during the first year.

West Side Forward has calculated that it would require ten to fifteen years of work and an investment of at least $1.9 billion to achieve these goals.[1] This is social entrepreneurship on a massive scale that requires the continuous influx of resources including capital, training, and community solidarity, over an extended period of time. In light of the required scope of the West Side Forward project, difficulties and setbacks faced by programs such as the West Side Xcelerator are not a sign of failure of the program, itself, nor of the idea of social entrepreneurship, but rather the lack of commitment to that idea by all parties, including investors, employers, and potential entrepreneurs.

This begs the question of why investors would be so reluctant to support programs like the West Side Xcelerator and West Side Forward. Certainly, the chapter thus far has shown that the challenges of overcoming inner city poverty are

---

[1] This information comes from a pamphlet provided to the authors during their 2017 interview with Marvin Austin. It is an eight page fold out informational brochure produced by West Side Forward and, while it lacks an identifying title or date, it provides a clear outline of their development plan, which was corroborated by Austin in the interview. Further information on West Side Forward can be found on their website at http://bethelnewlife.org/impact/west-side-forward/.

daunting, but social enterprises frequently invest in poverty stricken regions in other countries, often with great success and, although some of the specific challenges may differ, they are substantial, nonetheless. The success of a venture like the Ixtlan Group (see Chapter 9) is dependent on the comprehensiveness of its scope, including, training, wages, access to capital, political power, and resource control as opposed to the piecemeal approach used in many American programs. One significant possibility is that poor communities in other countries are perceived as culturally predisposed to a shared, holistic approach because of their values, while Americans are conditioned to have an individualistic attitude that would not be open to such an approach. While this is an undeniably essentialist attitude, to a certain extent, it may be true. However, one of the basic premises of social entrepreneurship involves moving away from a completely individualistic view of economics. It seems strange then that social enterprises should concentrate the bulk of their efforts in areas where this mindset is already somewhat established, while undersupporting areas where it is not.

In conclusion, it is not that social entrepreneurship is unsuited to the developed world, even a poor inner city environment, like Chicago's West Side. Rather, it is the lack of belief in, and commitment to, this idea that creates difficulties. The belief in American capitalist individualism creates a powerful barrier to successful social entrepreneurship at all levels. This leads to the lack of trust between entrepreneurs and suppliers or distributors, the willingness of community members to patronize businesses owned and staffed by outsiders, and the unwillingness of investors to provide the needed capital as they assume that the individualistic nature of the community members will make this a poor prospect. While inner city environments certainly contain many barriers to successful economic development and community building, perhaps the greatest challenge is the perception that they are not valid sites for social enterprise and investment. This creates a vicious cycle where such projects do not receive the needed support because it is assumed the projects will not be successful. This lack of support impairs the success of the projects that are undertaken, reinforcing the idea that entrepreneurial programs will not work in an inner city environment, justifying future lack of support. To have a chance to turn this trend around and create the virtuous cycle associated with social enterprise would require the level of investment on all fronts presented in a program like West Side Forward.

References

Austin, M., Harris, R., & Coleman, E. (2014). *Bethel business accelerator: West Side business sector, White Paper.* Chicago: Bethel New Life.

Austin, M. (2017, March 12). Personal interview.

Bethel New Life. (2016). *West Side business xcelerator.* Chicago, IL: Bethel New Life.

Durr, M., Lyons, T.S., & Lichtenstein, G.A. (2000). Identifying the unique needs of urban entrepreneurs: African American skill set development. *Race & Society* 3: 75–90.

Luhby, T. (2016). Chicago: America's most segregated city. CNN Money [online]. Retrieved from https://money.cnn.com/2016/01/05/news/economy/chicago-segregated/index.html. Accessed July 17, 2018.

Moser, W. (2018). The 1968 Chicago riots—Why the West Side? Chicago [online]. Retrieved from http://www.chicagomag.com/city-life/April-2018/The-1968-Chicago-Riots-Why-the-West-Side/. Accessed July 17, 2018.

Porter, M.E. (1995). The competitive advantage of the inner-city. *Harvard Business Review* May–June: 56–71.

Sepulveda, F. (2012). The difference between a business accelerator and a business incubator? *Inc.*

Retrieved from https://www.inc.com/fernando-sepulveda/the-difference-between-a-business-accelerator-and-a-business-incubator.html. Accessed May 17, 2018.

Shinnar, R.S., Aguilera, M.B., & Lyons, T.S. (2011). Co-ethnic markets: Financial penalty or opportunity? *International Business Review* 20(6): 646–658.

Semuels, A. (2018). Chicago's awful divide. The Atlantic [online]. Retrieved from https://www.theatlantic.com/business/archive/2018/03/chicago-segregation-poverty/556649/. Accessed July 17, 2018.

Young, J. (2014). A tale of two Chicagos: Violence plagues city's south, west sides. NBC News [online]. Retrieved from https://www.nbcnews.com/news/us-news/tale-two-chicagos-violence-plagues-citys-south-west-sides-n86166. Accessed July 17, 2018.

Chapter 7
An Example from Michigan:
The Michigan State University Product Center
Food-Ag-Bio

This chapter presents a case from the state of Michigan. It examines the work of a center within Michigan State University (MSU) that supports entrepreneurship in the agriculture and food sectors of the economy. In the course of its work, the MSU Product Center Food-Ag-Bio helps residents of the state build a business asset, irrespective of whether they are located in rural or urban areas, thereby contributing to wealth creation. Before we delve into MSU's Land Grant Mission and the programs and activities of the Product Center, it is useful to understand some basic Michigan demographics and the nature of Michigan agriculture and its food processing industry.

Michigan's estimated current total population is 9.99 million (World Population Review, 2018), and has remained roughly the same over the past fifteen years. The urban/rural population split is approximately 80 percent/20 percent. The rural population tends to be older than the urban on average, a situation that will exacerbate the continuing decline in that population. Households in rural areas have a lower median income as well—$51,538 in urban counties, $45,646 in mostly rural counties, and $38,145 in completely rural counties (McVicar, 2016). Michigan's rural median household income is substantially lower than that of the United States, which is $52,368, and the state's urban median household income is also lower than the country's figure (Tanner, 2016). Thus, this is a state that is not growing and tends to have lower income than the nation as a whole, particularly in its rural areas.

Agriculture plays a major role in Michigan's economy. It contributes $101.2 billion annually to that economy. It accounts for 22 percent of the state's employment. There are over 50,000 farms and approximately 10 million acres of farmland. Michigan's agricultural economy is the second most diverse in the United States, behind California. It produces over 300 commodities and leads the country in the production of dry beans, blueberries, pickling cucumbers, squash, and tart cherries. It is also a leader in floriculture and in the production of potatoes that are used for potato chip processing. Michigan has over 300 farmers markets, which ranks it third in the nation (MDARD, 2018; MARVAC, 2018).

The state is also a major exporter of agricultural commodities and food products, having exported $2.8 billion worth in 2015. The state's leading export markets are Canada, China, Japan, Mexico, and Thailand. Its chief exports are

DOI 10.1515/9781547400461-007

dairy products, feed and feed grains, processed food products, soybeans and soybean meal, and vegetables. For every $1 of export activity, another $2.93 in economic activity is generated (MDARD, 2018).

In the closely related food processing industry, the economic impact was estimated to be $25 billion at the time of the last Census in 2010. This industry was estimated to have created 134,000 jobs (Knudson et al., 2010).

MSU and the MSU Product Center

Founded in 1855, MSU was one of the first Land Grant universities established under the Morrill Act of 1852. The Act, sponsored by Vermont Congressman Justin Smith Morrill and signed into law by President Abraham Lincoln, set aside public land for the creation of "Colleges for the Benefit of Agriculture and the Mechanical Arts" (Library of Congress, 2018). These colleges were established to serve the children of working class families, who at the time did not have access to affordable higher education. They were an early attempt to mitigate wealth inequality in the United States through education.

In addition to making a college education more widely accessible, Land Grant universities are well known for their outreach to their communities and to the states in which they are located, largely through their Cooperative Extension (now just called Extension) programs. The idea is to bring the knowledge generated by the university's scholars to the public in a form upon which the latter can act.

It was in this environment of egalitarian higher education and a commitment to applied research and the community, that the MSU Product Center Food-Ag-Bio (hereafter referred to as the "Product Center" or "the Center") was born in 2003. It was the brainchild of Dr. H. Christopher Peterson and was founded with the support of the College of Agriculture and Natural Resources at MSU, the Michigan Agricultural Experiment Station program (now known as AgBioResearch) and Michigan State University Extension (MSUE). It still receives most of its funding from MSUE and AgBioResearch.

The mission of the Product Center is to support entrepreneurship in the food, value-added agriculture, and natural resource-based product sectors of the Michigan economy. The goal is to help properly motivated entrepreneurs in these sectors to start, grow, and sustain businesses in order to create wealth for themselves, their families, and their communities, contributing to the overall health of the Michigan economy. Originally, the majority of Product Center clients were small farmers who were looking for other sources of revenue because they were unable to make a living solely by selling their commodity crops. They needed help in creating products by adding value to their crops or livestock-based commodities and building businesses around these new products. As time went on, there was less demand for value added agricultural entrepreneurship, and the Product Center shifted its efforts toward helping any properly motivated would-be entrepreneur, located anywhere in Michigan, who wanted to create and sell a food or natural resource product.

Today, about 80 percent of the Product Center's clients make food products. These include jellies and jams, pasta sauce, salsa, baked goods, dessert toppings, a variety of meat and poultry products, fish products, packaged vegetables, beverages (coffee, tea, fruit sodas, etc.), confections, and a host of specialty foods. The other 20 percent make nonfood items, such as health and beauty products. The Product Center also works with food retailers and restaurants. Many of these entrepreneurs come from low-income communities and limited personal means; some are physically disabled.

The Product Center's Pipeline

The Product Center thinks of itself as managing a "pipeline of entrepreneurs and enterprises" (Lichtenstein & Lyons, 2010). By helping new entrepreneurs to develop their skills, the Center supports them to move their businesses more efficiently and effectively through their life cycle stages from pre-venture to maturity (see Figure 4.1 in Chapter 4). If managed well, this combined entrepreneurial activity can have a significant impact on the Michigan economy. To manage this pipeline efficaciously, the center must manage both volume and flow. In other words, the volume of entrepreneurial activity must be sufficient to have the potential to generate substantial impact, and clogs (a lack of progress by an entrepreneur and their enterprise) and breaks (business failure) in the pipeline must be addressed (Lichtenstein & Lyons, 2010). This model permits the Center to be strategic in the services it provides and the way in which its resources are deployed.

In order for the Product Center to carry out its pipeline approach, it must work with entrepreneurs at all levels of skill and every stage in the business life cycle. This is unusual among entrepreneurship support organizations (ESOs), many of which are moving toward a focus on growth companies because they create the most return in terms of jobs, income, and tax base. As Lichtenstein and Lyons (2010) point out, this is a form of skimming without taking responsibility for making more cream. The Product Center takes the position that investing in low-skilled entrepreneurs operating very early stage companies is not only essential to sustainable economic development, it can pay off handsomely over time in both economic returns and increased inclusivity in entrepreneurship as well.

The latter has a social benefit in that it uses markets to distribute wealth creation opportunity and capability more widely.

The Product Center's Structure

In order to be suitably comprehensive, the Product Center has developed a set of networks that reach across the MSU campus and the entire state. The Center, itself, is organized as a campus-based staff and a field staff. The campus staff is constituted of fifteen faculty members, industry specialists, and administrative professionals who bring a breadth of expertise to their work. Among the skill sets represented are business development, economic development, economic feasibility assessment, economic impact assessment, entrepreneurship, events planning and implementation, food safety, food science, market analysis, marketing, nutrition, packaging, and program/project evaluation.

The Product Center's field staff is known as the Innovation Counselors Network (ICN). When fully staffed, the ICN numbers eleven, scattered geographically across the state of Michigan (see Figure 7.1). These are Extension Educators who work for MSUE but spend 50 percent or more of their time assisting the Product Center's client entrepreneurs. They act as business coaches, engaging in longer-term relationships with their clients, as they move them from an idea to a sustainable business concept, help them to launch their business, and then help them to begin to grow it. The ICN mostly works with early stage entrepreneurs. No fees are charged for their assistance; although a modest application fee is charged to clients as they enter the Product Center system.

When the Innovation Counselors can not help client entrepreneurs themselves, they make referrals. Most of these are made to the campus staff, who work in two divisions of the Product Center—Specialized Services and Strategic Research. Specialized Services provides science-based assistance to client entrepreneurs in the areas of food safety, nutrition facts labeling, packaging, and sensory testing and other product development activities. Specialized Services relies on partnerships with other units on the MSU campus to deliver this assistance. These partners include the Department of Food Science and Human Nutrition; School of Packaging; Department of Agricultural, Food, and Resource Economics; and the College of Communication Arts, to name a few. Even students lend their expertise. In undergraduate capstone courses in Packaging and Food Industry Management, student teams provide insights to Product Center client entrepreneurs on packaging options and marketing and branding. This suite of services is arguably the Product Center's competitive advantage. There is no place else in Michigan where a food industry entrepreneur can get this degree of help all in one place.

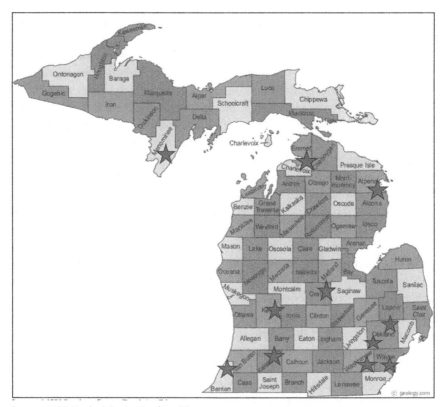

Source: MSU Product Center Food-Ag-Bio

Figure 7.1: Map of Innovation Counselor Locations Across Michigan

The Center's Strategic Research Group is constituted of four PhD-level econo-mists who assist clients with various forms of applied economics. Among these are market analysis, economic impact assessment, and feasibility assessment. There are modest fees charged for the assistance of both Specialized Services and the Strategic Research Group.

When no one within the Product Center or on the MSU campus can help a client, a referral is made to one of several external partners across the state. An example is assistance with the export of agricultural or food products. The Mich-igan Department of Agriculture and Rural Development (MDARD) has a strong exporting department. Many Center clients with a need for export assistance have been helped by MDARD, which provides exporting preparation services as well as assistance in reaching overseas markets.

For many of the clients of the Product Center, the ultimate achievement is to get their product sold in grocery store chains. Many start out making small amounts of their product in their home kitchen under the Michigan Cottage Food Law and selling it in small boutique food stores or at farmer's markets. These early stage entrepreneurs can get by making a few dozen units of their product, with a shelf life of eight–ten days; however, selling in a large grocery store requires the ability to produce substantially more volume and to make a product with a much longer shelf life. The Product Center provides help in making this major transition. It also makes connections between its client entrepreneurs and distributors or retailers. This might take place through the connections of an individual Innovation Counselor or via the Product Center's annual conference and marketplace trade show, called Making It in Michigan.

Making It in Michigan, as the name implies, focuses on advancing Michigan-made food products, whether made by Product Center clients or other food manufacturers. The conference portion of this one-day event, held at the convention center in downtown Lansing, passes current and relevant information and knowledge on to food entrepreneurs through educational sessions held throughout the morning of the event. Recent session topics have included a grocery buyers panel, a food distributors panel, food safety regulation, business finance, marketing to millennials, and food photography, to name a few. The tradeshow is the featured event of the afternoon. It typically includes between 175 and 210 food vendors, depending on the year, whose companies are Michigan-based. Many are Product Center clients; however, there are a considerable number of nonclients as well. Buyers from major food distributors and retailers walk the floor, sampling the vendors' products. This typically results in numerous contracts between the buyers' companies and the food makers, the ultimate goal of the event. One retailer holds an annual competition called "The Next SKU May Be You." The winners of this competition are three food vendors selected by the retailer to receive a year of free shelf space at their stores. Members of the public are also invited to attend the trade show and sample the vendors' products. Over the years, Making It in Michigan has grown significantly and has become the Product Center's signature event.

The beneficiaries of most of the services and events outlined above are lower-skilled entrepreneurs operating early-stage businesses. Because the Product Center works the entire pipeline of entrepreneurs and enterprises, it has clients whose skills are more advanced, as are their companies. Working with these clients requires a very different approach that must be sophisticated enough to meet their needs. The margin for error in assisting these clients is thin, as they will only continue to work with the Product Center if they feel they are receiving value. Yet, when it comes to wealth building, this particular form of assistance is crucial because wealth is created when entrepreneurial ventures grow. These entrepreneurs are moving into the growth stage of their enterprises.

The Center offers two suites of services to this group of entrepreneurs: Accelerated Growth Services (AGS) and the Food Processing and Innovation Center (FPIC). AGS offers business coaching for growth stage entrepreneurs. It also provides strategic planning assistance and help with meeting food safety regulations. In addition, the Product Center has plans for mobilizing partners on- and off-campus to create rapid response teams that help later stage businesses address complex problems as part of the AGS suite of services.

In its work with growth companies, the Product Center recognized a need among them that was not being met in Michigan or elsewhere. When a food company seeks to grow, they are typically looking to develop a new product line. This requires the facility, equipment, and capability to experiment. Yet, many smaller companies have none of these things. Unlike large companies, they can not afford a research and development (R&D) facility with state-of-the-art food processing equipment. They also can not afford the risk of putting everything they have into a new product and selling it into a market that rejects it. As a result, these young companies are stuck, unable to engage in the kind of innovation necessary for growth.

An example of this phenomenon would be a company that has established itself making fruit pies. Its pies are good, and they have served to establish the company's brand in the marketplace. The entrepreneur(s) behind this business sees an opportunity to introduce a meat pie to the market; however, the manufacture of this product brings a new set of challenges, among them food safety, packaging, and food science issues. Even if this meat pie is made successfully, will the market accept it?

It was this situation that the Product Center had in mind when it set out to create an innovation center for smaller growth-oriented food companies. One that would provide access to a facility with the latest equipment and all the food safety licenses and certifications to allow the product created there to be sold into the market in small batches, permitting the food maker to test the market and limit its exposure to risk. The result of this creative and innovative effort—the FPIC—opened its doors in March 2018, after six years in the making.

The FPIC is an 8,000 sq. ft. fully licensed food processing plant. It has a raw preparation area; a flexible snap in and out production line that allows the processor to choose the combination of equipment it will use; a packaging area; cold, frozen and dry storage; and a loading dock. It is capable of accommodating virtually any kind of food or beverage product, with the exception of alcoholic beverages. The latter is because the facility does not currently have the equipment for this type of production. This may change in the future.

The FPIC was built with a grant from the Economic Development Administration of the U.S. Department of Commerce, which was matched by the Michigan

Economic Development Corporation, Michigan Department of Agriculture and Rural Development and MSU. The total cost was approximately $5.8 million. The facility operates on a fee basis, with a daily fee for its use. Companies might use the FPIC for a single day or as many as ten days, depending on the product testing they need to do.

While the FPIC was built for use by small companies that are seeking to drive their own growth, an interesting and unanticipated phenomenon has emerged. Large food processors, distributors and retailers are showing interest in supporting the smaller industry "disruptors" in creating new products. The larger companies are hoping to either acquire these smaller businesses or bring them into their supply chains. This is reflective of a larger trend in the economy, as increasingly small, entrepreneurial ventures are the source of most disruptive innovation (Christensen et al., 2015). This is another way that entrepreneurship generates wealth through growth.

The Product Center and Wealth Inequality

The Product Center is arguably a social venture with a mission of supporting commercial entrepreneurs in the food, agriculture, and natural resource economic sectors to start, sustain, and grow their businesses, thereby building wealth. It meets Dees's (1998) criteria (discussed in Chapter 4) for such a venture in that it is mission driven. Over the course of its history, it has been opportunistic in its quest to serve its client entrepreneurs more effectively. The addition of the Making It in Michigan event to connect food makers to their markets in 2007, the move to provide a deeper relationship-based experience for clients through coaching in 2017, and the addition of the FPIC in 2018 are examples of this positive opportunism. The Product Center has acted as a learning organization—listening to its clients' needs and innovating to serve those needs. The Center has also been highly accountable for its impact on its clients and the economy of the state of Michigan. Since 2004, it has measured this impact and communicated it to its stakeholders, both inside and outside MSU. Table 7.1 provides output and outcome measures for Fiscal Year 2016–2017 and for the Product Center's history.

Table 7.1: Product Center Outputs and Outcomes, 2004–2017 and FY 2016–2017

Services Provided (Outputs)	2004–2017	FY 2016–2017
One-on-one client coaching	51,268 sessions	4, 164 sessions
Assistance with business concept development	4, 931 clients	476 clients
Venture start-ups (commencement or continuation or planning for a new business or an expansion for an existing business	2,551 clients	282 clients
Specialized services (includes product testing, market analysis, and feasibility studies)	2, 935 clients	389 clients
Venture launches (commencement of economic activity for new or existing businesses through new sales, investment, or employment	634 ventures	91 ventures

Assistance in Launching 634 ventures yielded the following estimated economic outcomes:
- Increased annual sales: $402.3 million (cumulative first year sales only)
- Value of increased investment: $425.3 million
- Jobs created: 1,995
- Jobs retained: 1,272

Source: Michigan State University Product Center Food-Ag-Bio 2017 Annual Report, "Growing Entrepreneurs and the Michigan Economy." East Lansing, MI.

Another approach to understanding the Product Center's impact is to look at some representative examples of clients and their companies. Because the center takes a "big tent" approach to assisting client entrepreneurs—it works with any individual or team in Michigan that has the necessary passion to start and grow a food, agriculture, or natural resource-based business—its client base is very diverse. There are women-owned and minority-owned businesses as well as companies owned by people with physical disabilities. There are entrepreneurs who start at different levels of skill and at different stages in the business life cycle; however, it is fair to say that the majority of the Product Center's clients begin their entrepreneurial journey with minimal skills and at the earliest stages of business development. Some are entrepreneurs by necessity, but the majority see an opportunity to add value by creating and selling a product that meets a customer need and desire. Many come from modest economic backgrounds.

When the Product Center first met Nialah Ellis-Brown in 2008, she was twenty years old and selling bottles of tea, made using her great-grandfather's hibiscus tea recipe, from the trunk of her car in Detroit. The tea was branded as Ellis Island Tropical Tea, a reflection of the fact that her great-grandfather was from Jamaica and entered the United States through Ellis Island (Edward, 2017; Purtan, 2017). The Center was able to help get her business going, which is now known as Ellis Infinity Beverage Company. Nialah became the only minority female beverage maker in the state of Michigan, a distinction she still holds (Sam's Club, 2017).

Since that time, Nialah has continued to grow her business. She has changed her brand to Ellis Island Jamaican Tea, which is carried in over 500 stores, including grocery chains Meijer, Michigan Kroger stores, Midwest Whole Foods Markets, and Sam's Clubs (Edward, 2017). In addition, HMSHost is selling her tea in its airport stores (Edward, 2017). All of this activity has allowed the Ellis Island Tea plant to move from operating one shift per week to running all five days a week (Purtan, 2017). In 2017, she was named to *Forbes* 30 Under 30 list.

While the great majority of Product Center clients are developing and operating businesses with a profit motive, there is a growing number of social entrepreneurs who are seeking assistance as well. One of these is Rebecca Cruttenden, the founder of Clara Cookies LLC, which is located in Rockford, MI, in the western part of the state.

Rebecca is an Ironman competition athlete, who uses this as a means for raising money for a charity she founded and directs called Team Orphans. This charity assists special needs abandoned children by providing adoption grants that support finding these children permanent families. As of 2017, Rebecca had raised over $200,000 for Team Orphans through her Ironman endeavors. Since 2010, she has been able to place forty children.

As an athlete, Rebecca was always looking for high-energy foods to fuel her through her competitions. She tells the story of growing tired of peanut butter sandwiches and deciding to make her own peanut butter chocolate chip protein cookies. She found that her family and friends enjoyed these cookies as much as she did. As a result, her husband encouraged her to build a business around them.

Rebecca began working with the Product Center to develop a marketing plan that focused on selling the cookies to athletes who championed social causes as well as to businesses that support athletes (e.g., sporting goods retailers). In 2016, she launched Clara Cookies as a for-profit venture with a social mission, raising all of her start-up funding ($17,000) through a Go-Fund-Me crowdfunding campaign. Rebecca named her company for an adopted special needs child in Wisconsin. She donates all of her after-tax profits to Team Orphans.

Clara Cookies' product is a large, individually wrapped cookie that is protein fortified and gluten free. It comes in four flavors: coconut dark chocolate chip, dark chocolate chip with almonds, lemon poppy-seed, and peanut butter chocolate chip. Customers buy these cookies as training food, a snack, or a convenient meal substitute.

At present, Clara Cookies operates out of a commercial kitchen at Camp Roger, an outdoor education and summer camp for children and families, which donates the space. The company relies on sixteen volunteers, which it calls the Clara Cookies Baking Team, to produce its product. It also uses volunteers to deliver the cookies to at least thirty locations for sale. One of her largest clients is Premier Food Service, which operates dining services in Fort Wayne, IN and Lansing, Mason and Rockford, MI. Rebecca is working to expand her market. In 2017, she received the Product Center Director's Award for her unique accomplishments at that year's Making It in Michigan event.

Another social entrepreneur who is a client of the Product Center is Kathy Sample, who operates Argus Farm Stop in Ann Arbor, MI.[1] Kathy formed Argus in 2014 to encourage the production and purchase of locally grown food by ensuring that farmers get a fair return on the food they sell.

In the traditional agri-food value chain, the farmer only receives, on average, less than 16 cents on the dollar (Dunnam, 2017). Kathy believes this can best be addressed by providing a marketplace in which farmers can sell directly to consumers. Argus Farm Stop provides such a place and works to maximize the share of sales received by farmers. At essence, it is a "fair trade" farmers market.

Argus Farm Stop accomplishes this through a daily, year-round farmers market that sells only locally grown food. Participating farmers retain ownership of their products and set their own prices. Argus staff sells these products, which are clearly identified by farm and growing method employed, using a consignment model. Eighty percent of sales revenue goes to the farmers.

Argus seeks to engage customers by creating an enjoyable shopping experience for them. There are opportunities to interact with farmers, and an on-site café serves as a gathering place. The revenue generated by the café also is used to offset the cost of operating the market.

When the market first opened, it had forty participating farmers. That number grew to over 200 by 2016. Argus estimates that their initial investment of $170,000 has returned over $2.2 million to date to the local farmers who participate. This has served to help keep local small farmers in business when they might otherwise have failed.

These examples demonstrate that the Product Center fosters entrepreneurship that helps to set individuals on a path to success. This success may be commercial or social, but it contributes to society and helps to mitigate wealth inequality either way.

---

1 The material for this example was derived from a presentation by Kathy Sample on Argus Farm Stop, Making It in Michigan Conference, Lansing, MI, November 7, 2017.

References

Christensen, C.M., Raynor, M.E., & McDonald, R. (2015). What is disruptive innovation? *Harvard Business Review*, December.

Dunnam, A. (2017). Farmers receive less than sixteen cents of the American food dollar. Retrieved from https://nfu.org/2017/09/22/farmers-receive-less-than-sixteen-cents-of-the-american-food-dollar/. Accessed May 16, 2018.

Edward, R. (2017). No title. *Michigan Chronicle*. Retrieved from https://michronicleonline.com/2017/06/21/188712/. Accessed May 16, 2018.

Knudson, W.A., Miller, S., & Peterson, H.C. (2010). The economic impact of the Michigan food processing industries. The Strategic Marketing Institute Working Paper 01-0910, September.

Library of Congress. (2018). Morrill Act. Retrieved from https://www.loc.gov/rr/programs/bib/ourdocs/Morrill.html. Accessed April 30, 2018.

Lichtenstein, G.A., & Lyons, T.S. (2010). *Investing in entrepreneurs: A strategic approach for strengthening your regional and local economy.* Santa Barbara, CA: Praeger/ABC-CLIO.

MARVAC. (2018). 10 impressive facts about Michigan's diverse agricultural industry. Retrieved from http://www.michiganrvandcampgrounds.org/10-facts-michigan-agriculture-ag-day/. Accessed July 2, 2018.

McVicar, B. (2016). Michigan's urban, rural divide on display in new Census data. *Michigan News*. Retrieved from https://www.mlive.com/news/index.ssf/2016/12/michigans_urban_rural_divide_0.html. Accessed July 2, 2018.

MDARD. (2018). Facts about Michigan agriculture. Retrieved from https://michigan.gov/mdard/0,4610,7-125-1572-7775--,00.html. Accessed July 2, 2018.

Purtan, J. (2017). Mom's a genius update: Detroit tea company goes nationwide. Retrieved from http://www.wxyz.com/money/consumer/dont-waste-your-money/moms-a-genius/moms-a-genius-update-detroit-tea-company-takes-sales-nationwide. Accessed May 16, 2018.

Sam's Club Staff. (2017). When big business and small business work together, it's teariffic. Retrieved from https://corporate.samsclub.com/blog/2017/09/14/when-big-businessses-and-small-businesses-work-together-its-teariffic. Accessed May 16, 2018.

Tanner, K. (2016). Census: Michigan's rural areas top urban areas in income, home values. *Detroit Free Press*. Retrieved fromhttps://www.freep.com/story/opinion/contributors/raw-data/2016/12/08/census-new-data-outline-urban-rural-divide/95085072/2/. Accessed July 2, 2018.

World Population Review (2018). Michigan population 2018. Retrieved from http://worldpopulationreview.com/states/michigan-population/. Accessed July 2, 2018.

Chapter 8
An Example from Poland:
The Warsaw Entrepreneurship Forum

Warsaw is the largest city in Poland, with a population of over 1.7 million, and is that country's seat of government. It has an area of approximately 200 square miles. It ranks in the top five among European capitals for foreign investment and is second only to Moscow in terms of anticipated foreign investment in the next few years. The city ranks among the top three of European metropolitan areas for its attractiveness for entrepreneurship. In addition, 30 percent of all of the companies in Poland that have foreign investment have their headquarters in Warsaw (Center for Entrepreneurship, 2014).

Poland was under communist rule for almost fifty years, as part of the Soviet Bloc. When the communist system collapsed in 1989, the country took the opportunity to transform its government and its economy. It became a democracy, with a parliamentary system and competitive elections. It adopted a new constitution in 1997 that created a two-party parliament and a multi-party republic. It became increasingly relevant and active in Europe's political and economic events (Marked by Teachers, n.d.).

In 1990, the Polish government undertook the highly ambitious effort to convert its economy from the communist model of state ownership and central planning to the capitalist model with mostly private ownership and resources allocated by markets. This effort was known as the Balcerowicz Plan. It attempted to quickly deregulate prices, end shortages, stop subsidies to state enterprises, deregulate foreign trade, control inflation, and align the Polish currency with other currencies. Poland began trading extensively with Europe and the United States (Marked by Teachers, n.d.).

At first, many of the maladies of unfettered capitalism were experienced—high unemployment, poverty and the creation of socioeconomic classes. In 2008, an economic boom began, and there was a reversal of many of these issues, aided by government intervention that was less restrictive than it had been under communism but essential to protecting society. Civil rights were secured, as was free speech. The media was no longer state controlled. Nongovernmental organizations began to proliferate (Marked by Teachers, n.d.; King & Sznajder, 2003).

In this milieu of a transitioning economy and society, the Warsaw Entrepreneurship Forum was conceived and implemented. It ran for just over two years, from September 2012 to October 2014, and was designed to foster entrepreneurship in the districts of central Warsaw.

DOI 10.1515/9781547400461-008

The Warsaw Entrepreneurship Forum

Entrepreneurship in Poland exploded after 1989. The country has 3.5 million registered businesses; 1.7 million of these are active. The majority (68 percent) are sole proprietorships (no employees). In Warsaw, there are 158,539 active companies. Sixty-six percent of these companies were founded since 2001 (Center for Entrepreneurship, 2014; Cieslik, n.d.). Despite this high degree of activity, researchers discovered several key weaknesses in Warsaw's entrepreneurship field (Cieslik, 2012):

- Awareness and contact between local business owners was very low to non-existent.
- Contact between entrepreneurs and local government officials was very limited, with no platforms for entrepreneurs to express their needs and concerns.
- Local government lacked the data and tools to effectively foster entrepreneurship.
- Local government had no trained staff who could serve as liaison to the business community.

More specifically, researchers at Kozminski University in Warsaw found that entrepreneurs in that city not only did not know each other, they did not cooperate. In fact, they deliberately chose not to cooperate, failing to see its benefit. In many respects, they represented the old adage that recent converts to a paradigm are usually its greatest zealots. As newly minted capitalists, they believed that competition was the answer to all business questions (Cieslik, n.d.).

These weaknesses speak to a lack of networking, among entrepreneurs and between government and entrepreneurs, and a local government that was ill prepared to support entrepreneurship successfully. Addressing these shortcomings became the focus of the Warsaw Entrepreneurship Forum. Before describing the forum, itself, we examine the topics of networking and the role of government in fostering entrepreneurship.

Networking and Social Capital

The ability to network is widely considered a crucial skill necessary for successful entrepreneurship. Entrepreneurs need to be able to develop and manage relationships, both within their companies and in the larger context in which they operate (Lyons & Lyons, 2015). Networking carries with it several key advantages (Neck et al., 2018):

- Access to role models and mentors
- Access to diverse and complementary skillsets
- Trust building that potentially leads to access to private information
- Risk mitigation through information and advice
- Emotional support for isolated entrepreneurs
- Power created through unity that can be leveraged

Social capital building is at the heart of networking. This is the intentional creation of connections between and among individuals and organizations. While social capital is intangible, economists consider it a legitimate form of capital, on the same level as physical, human, and financial capital. This is because, like these other forms of capital, it adds value (Neck et al., 2018). It can improve productive action (Coleman, 1988).

Social capital is often thought of as being comprised of three dimensions. The *structural* dimension has to do with the nature of the social connections, or "ties" created. These ties are characterized as being either "strong" or "weak." Strong ties might be thought of as formal connections, while weak ties are informal connections (Lyons et al., 2012). Strong ties tend to perpetuate the status quo; weak ties foster creativity and innovation (Lyons, 2002). For this reason, networks of weak ties are believed to be the best social capital structure for encouraging successful entrepreneurship (Fortunato & Alter, 2011).

The *relational* dimension of social capital has to do with trust. Trust is built through integrity and reciprocity. The former is doing what you say you will do. The latter has to do with paying back a favor received. Lin (1999: 30) has observed that social capital can be described as "investment in social relations with expected returns."

The third dimension of social capital is *cognitive*. As the name implies, it has to do with the way people think about each other and their commonalities. To what degree do they share beliefs, values and a vision? (Neck et al., 2018). The more they have in common, the stronger the bond.

Putnam (2000) makes a useful structural distinction regarding social capital. He argues that there are essentially two important types: bonding and bridging. Bonding social capital builds unity and identity within a group. Bridging social capital develops links between one group and others outside that group. The former is exclusive and creates solidarity. The latter is inclusive and supports the sharing and exchange of ideas and resources, enabling reciprocity (Putnam, 2000: 22–23). In entrepreneurship, bonding social capital is helpful to bringing the members of a team operating an enterprise together around a brand or a mission, while bridging social capital links that enterprise to partners, providers of support, suppliers, and so forth in that enterprise's ecosystem.

The Role of Government in Fostering Entrepreneurship

In recent years, it has become widely accepted that government should play a role in encouraging entrepreneurial activity. Chapter 3 of this book explores this phenomenon as an economic development strategy. How this role is played remains a matter for debate. Part of the problem is that government tends to operate very differently than entrepreneurs. It is typically bureaucratic, slow to act, and risk averse. While this may be appropriate to the role it must play, it is antithetical to successful entrepreneurship. Given this, it is argued that government's role must be indirect.

At the beginning of this movement to engage government with entrepreneurship, government played the role of provider of resources—business training, technical training, access to information, and financing. To some extent, it still plays this role. However, some have challenged this as not being sufficient to advance entrepreneurship in a significant way. Resources are only useful when the entrepreneur is prepared to use them effectively (Lichtenstein & Lyons, 1996). Entrepreneurs are not all the same in terms of their capability; therefore, resources should be matched to the skill level of the entrepreneur (Lichtenstein & Lyons, 2010).

In light of these criticisms, governments have stepped back in their efforts to foster entrepreneurship into a role that might best be described as facilitative. They coordinate the conditions that are conducive to successful entrepreneurship. They facilitate the activities of the myriad nonprofit, private and public entities in the given community that support entrepreneurship. They provide the soft (e.g., education) and hard (e.g., roadways, broadband) infrastructures that make business activity possible (Feldman, 1994). In this way, governments become the overseers of the local entrepreneurial ecosystem. Even then, they are not necessarily the direct liaison with entrepreneurs. Many communities, such as Buenos Aires in Argentina, have learned that it is best to have an entrepreneur in this latter role because entrepreneurs trust and respect other entrepreneurs (Lyons, 2014).

Partners in the Warsaw Entrepreneurship Forum

In response to the weaknesses in Warsaw's entrepreneurial ecosystem described earlier in this chapter, a partnership was created to address them. The two partner organizations were Kozminski University and the Warsaw Municipality.

The Warsaw Municipality was the lead partner in the Forum. It is the local government for the city of Warsaw, which is a city of just over 1.7 million people and 517.24 square kilometers (World Population Review, 2018). The city has been divided into eighteen districts.

Kozminski University is a private business and law institution of higher education located in Warsaw. It was founded in 1993 and currently enrolls 5,300 students. It offers degrees at the bachelors, masters, and doctoral levels. The largest program is the BA in management with an entrepreneurship major (Cieslik, 2017). Kozminski is also the home of the Center for Entrepreneurship, which was the principal representative of the university in this partnership.

The EU European Structural Fund supported the efforts of this partnership.

The Project

At its essence, the focus of the Warsaw Entrepreneurship Forum was the creation of an entrepreneur network in each of the six pilot districts of the eighteen total city districts (see Figure 8.1). The pilot districts selected were home to 38.6 percent of the total number of businesses located in Warsaw. The pilot project lasted twenty-five months, from October 2012 to October 2014 (Center for Entrepreneurship, 2014). The overall goal was to create a template for fostering interaction among entrepreneurs and between entrepreneurs and the Warsaw Municipality that could be transferred to the remaining twelve districts in the city.

Figure 8.1: Warsaw Entrepreneurship Forum entrepreneur network pilot districts

In support of this goal, the community–university partnership engaged in a set of inter-related activities (see Table 8.1). Kozminski University began the process by conducting preliminary research designed to determine the needs of the entrepreneurs in the six pilot districts and the extent to which they interacted with each other and with local government at the time of the Forum's launch. This research identified the weaknesses in the entrepreneurship field noted earlier in this chapter. The university also created a database that managed information on participating entrepreneurs, facilitated analysis of business activity by district, enabled communication with selected entrepreneurs, and monitored the status and progress of activities (Center for Entrepreneurship, 2014).

Table 8.1: Warsaw Entrepreneurship Forum: Summary of Activities and Outcomes

Key Activities	Key Outcomes
Research	Participation by 6,000 companies
Training of municipal staff	Several entrepreneur networks created
Electronic portals for entrepreneurs	Entrepreneurship skills improved
Networking meetings and coaching	Municipal staff trained in working with business
Building database	Policy tools for fostering entrepreneurship developed (reports and strategies)
Designing policy making tools	Systems/practices in place for deployment to remaining 12 districts of Warsaw
Dissemination of best practices	

Source: Center for Entrepreneurship (2014). Project: Warsaw entrepreneurship forum: Building local entrepreneurial community. Warsaw, Poland: Kozminski University.

Annual reports were produced, which chronicled the business situation in each of the six pilot districts. In addition, the university worked with the local government to develop an entrepreneurship promotion strategy. One of the key activities of the project was hiring, training and supporting six "liaison officers," one for each district. Their role was to represent the municipal government and foster interaction with participating entrepreneurs in the district (Center for Entrepreneurship, 2014).

An electronic portal was created for each district. These platforms were designed to encourage exchanges between entrepreneurs and facilitate the discussion of policy that affects entrepreneurship, which was valuable to officials of the Warsaw Municipality who were tasked with fostering entrepreneurial activity in the city (Center for Entrepreneurship, 2014).

The centerpiece of each entrepreneur network was the monthly meeting that brought the entrepreneurs of the district together. These meetings took place on weekday evenings and were about two hours in duration. A guest speaker was invited to discuss a topic of general interest to the entrepreneurs. Ample time was reserved for interactive discussion and the sharing of information among entrepreneurs. A moderator provided by Kozminski University, often a professor of entrepreneurship, led these interactive sessions. Additional facilitated meetings were held on topics of special interest to many entrepreneurs, an example being exporting (Center for Entrepreneurship, 2014). Municipal officials were always in attendance at these meetings, making themselves inconspicuous but available for answering questions and offering assistance. The process made government officials keenly aware that if they wanted the Forum to succeed, they needed to allow the entrepreneurs to run it.

Business development assistance was also provided to participating entrepreneurs through peer coaching. As an extension of this, workshops and seminars on best practices were convened routinely. The community–university partners made sure that these events included the latest practices from communities around the globe (Center for Entrepreneurship, 2014).

The Warsaw Entrepreneurship Forum culminated in an international conference held in Warsaw in July 2014. The conference spanned two days. The first involved practitioners and policymakers, who discussed the Forum itself, and its implications for fostering entrepreneurship in Warsaw and other urban communities. The second day brought together scholars from across Poland and elsewhere in Europe as well as the United States. Papers were presented and experiences shared relative to international efforts to encourage entrepreneurship. In particular, representatives of the cities in the Union of Polish Metropolises were urged to participate, as a means of sharing information and experiences.

Outcomes of the Warsaw Entrepreneurship Forum

The Forum accomplished several key outcomes (see Table 8.1). The entrepreneurs behind 6,000 companies located in the six pilot districts participated. These entrepreneurs experienced appreciable improvement in their skills because of the coaching offered by Kozminski University. Networking activities resulted in the creation of several entrepreneur networks and association that continued after the projects conclusion in October 2014.

Through the Forum's training initiative, staff of the Warsaw Municipality developed skills in successfully interacting with the local business community.

These skills were crucial to the government's goals for stimulating entrepreneurship in the future. During the course of the pilot project, numerous policy tools designed to facilitate the growth of entrepreneurship in the city were designed and produced. These included databases, business activity reports, and strategy reports. Among these was a tool for measuring changes in the city's level of entrepreneurial activity, dubbed the Warsaw Entrepreneurship Barometer. With an eye to transferring the work accomplished in the six pilot districts to the city's remaining districts, practices and systems were prepared.

Implications for Mitigating Wealth Inequality

Poland's transition from communism to capitalism brought some interesting challenges regarding both the interactions among businesses and the relationship between government and business. Warsaw entrepreneurs appeared to assume that the only relationship between businesses in a capitalist economy is a competitive one. To them, collaboration smacked of a reversion to communism. They had difficulty understanding that sometimes a company is better positioned to compete when it cooperates with other companies. Brandenburg and Nalebuff (1996) have called this "co-opetition." This is particularly true when businesses are very new and/or very small. They need protection from the challenges created by markets until they are strong enough to face these threats on their own.

For its part, the Warsaw Municipality was struggling with its new role. In a communist state, government runs businesses; in a capitalist economy, it facilitates their activities. The municipality had no experience in the latter and did not know how to reach out to businesses without being threatening to them or appearing to dictate policy without consulting them.

For both groups, this was a learning experience. Entrepreneurs came to understand the benefits of networking with peers. The local government learned how to listen to business people and allow them to take the lead in driving policy that encourages entrepreneurship. As one senior government official put it, "I think we have learned that it is best to let the entrepreneurs lead." This is why a partnership between local government and a university was beneficial in this case. Kozminski University could ably play the role of educator. They could guide their government partner to a project design that allowed the latter to play an appropriate role in the process and become comfortable in that role. By creating both in person and virtual opportunities for networking among entrepreneurs and ensuring the relevance of those interactions, the university could teach the value of co-opetition. An intersectoral partnership proved to be the ideal social enterprise for facilitating this effort to transform the city's economy through entrepreneurship.

The idea behind the Warsaw Entrepreneurship Forum is simple, but powerful. If entrepreneurs are given the opportunity to network among themselves, they will support each other, enhance their businesses, and, consequently, benefit the community's economy.

Underlying this strategy is the concept of entrepreneur networks, a form of social capital building. Research has shown that when entrepreneurs are brought together in peer groups, their interaction can yield numerous benefits. Chief among these is access to information, particularly private information—that which cannot be found in public sources (e.g., databases). The reason that this information is shared is the trust that is created through the social capital that is built via the networking process (Neck et al., 2018).

Another benefit flowing from entrepreneur networks is emotional support. Entrepreneurs tend to be isolated in their work, particularly when they are sole proprietors, as was the case with the great majority of entrepreneurs in Warsaw. A network relieves this sense of psychological isolation, acting as a substitute for the types of interaction intrinsic to larger organizations (Kutzhanova et al., 2009; Neck et al., 2018).

Networks provide access to skills a single entrepreneur may not have. This is helpful in solving problems. In a study of peer entrepreneur coaching groups in the Central Appalachian region of the United States, it was found that entrepreneurs often thought of their peer group as an advisory board to their company (Kutzhanova et al., 2009). The advice given in networks can be invaluable to reducing business risk. Networks have also helped entrepreneurs to identify role models and/or individuals with complementary skillsets who they can add to their management teams (Neck et al., 2018).

Networks are also a source of power in the sense that they allow individuals or small groups to accomplish more than they could alone (Neck et al., 2018). One of the reasons that the Warsaw Entrepreneurship Forum sought to create networks by district is that it was hoped that linking entrepreneurs together in each geographic sector of the city would make them more visible to the local government and give them a unified voice in advocating for policies that supported their efforts. This was further enhanced by creating the role of the district liaison officer.

Wealth inequality was addressed through entrepreneurship in this case because the social entrepreneurs who initiated and guided this effort elected to take a broad, nonexclusive approach to identifying participating entrepreneurs. While it is true that the city–university partnership was especially keen to support "high-technology" entrepreneurship because of its widely documented economic development benefits (Center for Entrepreneurship, 2014b), participation was open to all enterprises in the six pilot districts, thereby expanding opportunity.

The great majority of entrepreneurs who participated in the networks operated sole proprietorships. If left to their own devices, likely very few of these enterprises would have grown into engines of wealth creation, remaining, instead, forms of job and income substitution. In this respect, these were "prospective" entrepreneurs, given the definition of entrepreneurship employed in this book. However, because of the opportunities afforded by the social capital building in this case, many more of these entrepreneurs can reach their potential for growth.

Warsaw Entrepreneurship Forum Follow-Up

The Warsaw Entrepreneurship Forum was a two-year pilot project ending in 2014. A follow-up was conducted in 2018 to find out what longer-term impact the project had on efforts to advance entrepreneurship in the city. Of the six pilot districts, only one, Targowek, continued to fund its liaison officer. The remaining districts determined that they could not afford to sustain this position once the European Union funds were exhausted. Targowek's action has kept the entrepreneur and entrepreneur/municipality networks alive and has ensured the continued engagement of Kozminski University (Cieslik, 2018).

Staff from Kozminski's Center for Entrepreneurship participate regularly in entrepreneur network meetings and events. In cooperation with the Warsaw government, the university completed a three-year study of the goals and objectives of newly registered business owners in Targowek district. Approximately 2500 entrepreneurs responded to the survey questionnaire (Cieslik, 2018).

The Forum also had two broader impacts on entrepreneurship in Warsaw (Cieslik, 2018):
- The 2015 edition of the guide for newly elected counsellors in local governments included a chapter on supporting local entrepreneurship written by Kozminski University entrepreneurship professor Jerzy Cieslik. This guide is a regular publication of the Foundation for the Development of Local Democracy.
- In 2017, Kozminski's Center for Entrepreneurship was asked to advise the Supreme Audit Office (NIK) on how to design an audit of the efforts of local governments that promote entrepreneurship. The results of this audit are scheduled to be released in late 2018. The NIK is an independent state auditing body that seeks to safeguard public spending in Poland.

While the desired spread of entrepreneurship support across all of Warsaw's districts was not achieved in the short term, the work of the Warsaw Entrepreneurship Forum has continued on a smaller scale. As entrepreneurial successes continue in Targowek district, and are documented, other districts may come to recognize the value of investing in entrepreneur networks. It is also encouraging that the Forum's work has influenced thinking at the national level.

References

Brandenburger, A.M., & Nalebuff, B.J. (1996). *Co-Opetition*. New York: Broadway Business.

Center for Entrepreneurship. (2014a). Project: Warsaw entrepreneurship forum: Building local entrepreneurial community. Warsaw, Poland: Kozminski University.

Center for Entrepreneurship. (2014b). Entrepreneurial cities project directory. Warsaw, Poland: Kozminski University.

Cieslik. (2018). E-mail correspondence with Professor Jerzy Cieslik of Kozminski University, July.

Cieslik, J. (2017). Kozminski University: Developing minds for ambitious entrepreneurship and training teachers at other universities. In Volkmann, C.K., & Audretsch, D.B. (Eds.). *Entrepreneurship Education at Universities* (pp. 171–196). Cham: Springer.

Cieslik, J. (2012). Project: Warsaw entrepreneurship forum: Building local entrepreneurial community. Warsaw, Poland: Kozminski University, Center for Entrepreneurship.

Cieslik, J. (n.d.). "Warsaw entrepreneurship forum project." Interdisciplinary seminar at Kozminski University, Warsaw, Poland.

Coleman, J.S. (1988). Social capital in the creation of human capital. *American Journal of Sociology* 94 (Supplement): S95–S119.

Feldman, M.P. (1994). The university and economic development: The case of Johns Hopkins University and Baltimore. *Economic Development Quarterly* 8 (1): 67–76.

Fortunato, M. W-P., & Alter, T.R. (2011). The individual-institutional-opportunity nexus: An integrated framework for analyzing entrepreneurship development. *Entrepreneurship Research Journal* 1 (1): Article 6.

King, L., & Sznajder, A. (2003). Poland's state led transition to liberal capitalism. White paper. New Haven, CT: Yale University.

Kutzhanova, N., Lyons, T.S., & Lichtenstein, G.A. (2009). Skill-based development of entrepreneurs and the role of personal and peer group coaching in enterprise development. *Economic development Quarterly* 23 (3): 180––210.

Lin, N. (1999). Building a network theory of social capital. *Connections* 22 (1): 28–51.

Lyons, T.S. (2002). Building social capital for rural enterprise development: Three case studies in the United States. *Journal of Development Entrepreneurship* 7 (2): 193–216.

Lyons, T.S. (2014). Buenos Aires: Emerging entrepreneurial city. Retrieved from https://www.kozminski.edu.pl/fileadmin/wspolne_elementy/Jednostki/sfop/Artykuly_expertow/10_Buenos_Aires_Emerging_Entrepreneurial_City.pdf. Accessed July 9, 2018.

Lyons, T.S., Alter, T.R., Audretsch, D., & Augustine, D. (2012). Entrepreneurship and community: The next frontier of entrepreneurship inquiry. *Entrepreneurship Research Journal* 2 (1): Article 1.

Lyons, T.S., & Lyons, J.S. (2015). A skills assessment approach for operationalizing entrepreneur skill theory. White paper. Morristown, NJ: LEAP LLC.

Marked by Teachers. (n.d.). The change in Poland over the past 20 years: Communism to capitalism. Retrieved http://www.markedbyteachers.com/as-and—a-level/history/the-change-in-poland-over-the-past-20-years-communism-to-capitalism.html. Accessed May 24, 2018.

Neck, H.M., Neck, C.P., & Murray, E.L. (2018). *Entrepreneurship: The practice and mindset.* Los Angeles: Sage.

Putnam, R.D. (2000). *Bowling alone: The collapse and revival of American community.* New York: Simon and Schuster.

World Population Review. (2018). Warsaw Population 2018. Retrieved from http://worldpopulationreview.com/world-cities/warsaw-population/. Accessed June 12, 2018.

Chapter 9
Community Entrepreneurship: The Cases of the Lumber Enterprise in Ixtlan, Mexico, and the Pubs of Rural Ireland

To explore the variety of ways that social entrepreneurship manifests itself, this chapter looks at two very different instances of the practice. One is an intentionally created system of community-based businesses in a rural Mexican village. The other is a fixture of economic and social life in Ireland, which has evolved organically over the course of the past one hundred years or so. Despite their very different origins and trajectories, both systems face challenges relating to interactions with the world outside the community. Looking at these two case studies can provide insight into the nature of these challenges, regardless of whether the system profits or suffers from the interaction.

The first social entrepreneurship system examined here is the Ixtlan Group, a forestry and timber company run communally by a village of the Zapotec people in Mexico, examined by Mario Vazquez Maguirre, Gloria Camacho Ruelas, and Consuelo Garcia de la Torre in their article "Women Empowerment through Social Innovation in Indigenous Social Enterprises." Various groups of indigenous peoples make up 14.3 percent of the total Mexican population, with the Zapotec being the third largest of these groups. Among their communities are mountain villages in the Oaxaca region, of which Ixtlan is one. These native groups are protected by law under the Mexican government and usually own land communally rather than individually (Maguirre et al., 2016: 171). Such groups also tend to favor a form of communal governance known as *usos y costumbres* of which a major element is the assembly of the *comuneros* or community members, where all vote to elect officials and make decisions about community governance and resource use (Maguirre et al., 2016: 171–172).

While this form of governance does represent distinct advantages for building a system of social enterprise, it also can raise concerns regarding the empowerment and inclusion of certain subdivisions of the community. In this case, elements of traditional Mexican culture exert practical and social pressures that discourage women from participating in the assembly of *comuneros* or holding elected office, which significantly reduces their ability to have a voice in the direction their community will take or how valuable resources will be used. Thus, the experience of the Ixtlan group serves as a valuable model for how social enterprises can not only benefit the community as a whole but also serve as a powerful tool for equalizing these marginalized sections of the community.

DOI 10.1515/9781547400461-009

The village of Ixtlan conforms to these trends for communities of native peoples, holding the resources of the region and operating under the *usos y costumbres* system of governance. In the 1940s, Ixtlan switched its primary economic activity from agriculture to forestry in response to pressures from external businesses that harvested the local timber while providing very little benefit to the residents of the village in return. Community members from a number of native communities began to resist this kind of exploitation in the late 1960s. This eventually led to the government passing legislation in 1974 to protect the rights and resources of native peoples, empowering them to form their own businesses to utilize the resources on their land, rather than allowing exploitation by outside firms (Maguirre et al., 2016: 172). This laid the foundations for the organization that evolved into the modern Ixtlan Group, designed to provide employment to community members through the harvesting and use of local timber, while at the same time working to maintain the stability of the environment so the forests can remain a viable source of income for future generations. This organization also provides other benefits to the community, such as loans both for business enterprises and for personal/community life events like weddings, training, and empowerment for women, in the form of increased influence and leadership roles both in the company and in community governance.

This creates a complex structure of interlocking levels of social entrepreneurship, as the timber business run by the Ixtlan Group is, itself, a community business managed by the local assembly of *comuneros*, which makes the decisions regarding the use of local resources. In addition, it also serves as a support structure for other local businesses. Employees of the Ixtlan Group have access to management training as well as loans at low to no interest, which can serve as valuable tools for starting their own side businesses (Maguirre et al., 2016: 175, 177). Moreover, as the company operates on a policy of purchasing supplies locally whenever possible, it serves as a strong supporter of both new and existing businesses in the region (Maguirre et al., 2016: 176).

The activities of the Ixtlan Group create greater prosperity in the community and ensure that members get their basic needs met. Through the provision of fair and competitive employment, it provides "social security, housing credit, a pension, paid vacations and a Christmas bonus" (Maguirre et al., 2016: 175) as well as job security, as the Ixtlan Group makes it a policy never to fire any of the workers (Maguirre et al., 2016: 176). This sense of financial stability benefits the economy of the region as a whole and provides members with the sense of security needed to invest in ventures of their own.

The article by Maguirre, Ruelas, and de la Torre is focused primarily on the role the Ixtlan Group plays in empowering the women in the region, a role that is connected to its other functions as a social enterprise. As these authors point out, "women empowerment and social innovations reinforce each other in a virtuous circle (initial social innovations empower women in the organization, and these women also generated more social innovations) to increase productivity and growth in the social enterprise. The organic growth generates resources to address the economic, social, and environmental dimension of the social entity and its stakeholders, boosting sustainable community wellbeing" (Maguirre et al., 2016: 169).

Maguirre et al.'s study aims to measure the Ixtlan Group's impact on women in the area based on John Foley's system of five dimensions of empowerment: "democratic, economic, political, environmental, cultural" (Maguirre et al., 2016: 169). Information on this aspect of the organization was collected via interviews with thirty-nine men and thirty-one women, most of whom work for the Ixtlan Group, though a sampling was also included from other subgroups associated with the organization such as suppliers, clients, retirees, government officials, and other community members. Interviews averaged fifty minutes and were recorded in transcript form for data extraction. Subjects were questioned about the impact of the country on the economy, the environment, and social life of the area. Additional data was obtained via observation of the Ixtlan Group facilities for 120 hours and life in the village of Ixtlan for 200 hours (Maguirre et al., 2016: 170).

As has already been discussed, one of the main places gender inequality can be observed is the *comuneros* assembly that makes decisions for the community. Lack of female representation here limits empowerment in all aspects of life because the assembly has influence, or even direct control, over so many aspects of the village, including many of the operations of the Ixtlan Group. This confirms the argument that, "The main challenge that social enterprises face is to design governance mechanisms and structures that enhance the realization of equitable tasks in order to promote community well-being" (Maguirre et al., 2016: 167). Like many other such assemblies, the one at Ixtlan was exclusively male at the time of the Group's foundation, and it remained that way for nearly twenty years afterward. It is important to note that there was never an official rule preventing women from joining the assembly. Rather, they were kept out by social stigmas against their participation and by practical limitations, such as the assembly meeting during times when the women needed to provide childcare.

Despite these barriers, in the 1990s a small group of women demanded the right to participate in the assembly, opening the door for others to follow. Yet, numbers remain small as pressures against female participation, though reduced, are still in operation. At the time of the Maguirre et al. article's writing, women only held twenty-eight of the 384 seats in the assembly. On the other hand, the women who do choose to attend participate fully in the activities of government, rather than being silent observers, as is the case in some of the other local assemblies in the region (Maguirre et al., 2016: 173–174).

One of the main reasons that the women of the community have been able to challenge the barriers to their participation in local government is because the activities of the Ixtlan Group have provided them with empowerment in other aspects of their lives. These include both raw economic advantages and a greater sense of competency and control, both of which are considered key aspects of social enterprise because, "The empowerment of actors outside and inside the organizational boundaries seems to be one of the main characteristics of social entrepreneurship that differentiates it from other fields. This implies that social entrepreneurs usually create mechanisms and tools that both reduce the stakeholders' dependencies on the organization, and increase the stakeholders' abilities to contribute to the solution and to their own welfare" (Maguirre et al., 2016: 167).

The Ixtlan Group seeks to treat women with near total equality. Seventy employment positions in timber extraction in the area have been designated for men only because the community has not yet been able to purchase modern tools for this purpose, and the traditional means of performing this task is too physically demanding for most of the women (Maguirre et al., 2016: 179). Apart from this small exception, women receive the same salary and the same benefits of job security, bonuses, training, opportunities for promotion, and loans described previously as do the men (Maguirre et al., 2016: 177).

Financial security is crucial for female empowerment because when women remain dependent on men for their economic wellbeing, they can not challenge them for a role in government as the women of Ixtlan did. The policies of the Ixtlan Group have enabled women to prosper within the company as well as to start their own businesses, creating the solid financial footing necessary to agitate for political and cultural change. While the number of women in the assembly is still small, rapid economic gains for women imply this may soon change. In the past twenty years, the number of female employees in the Ixtlan Group has risen by 16 percent (Maguirre et al., 2016: 178). Women also operate 37.5 percent of the businesses in the community and are the primary breadwinners for 31.3 percent of the households (Maguirre et al., 2016: 177). The benefits of these changes are immediately evident. In addition to women's increasing role in local government, there have also been important social changes, such as the increasing acceptance of single motherhood, which is very unusual among the communities in the region (Maguirre et al., 2016: 181).

The Ixtlan Group is an excellent example of the quintessential modern social enterprise. It was deliberately engineered from the ground up, carefully constructed to provide specific economic and social benefits and it is relatively recent, owing its inception to the raising of social consciousness in the 1960s. It also fits the conventional ideas about social enterprises in that it involves a community of native people who, as shown in the previous chapter, are perceived as being more cooperative and less individualist than members of modern society. As Maguirre, Ruelas, and de la Torre claim, "Social enterprises in indigenous communities are recognized as highly effective, because the cultural characteristics of this type of communities facilitate the establishment of this type of enterprises" (Maguirre et al., 2016: 167).

Yet, it is important to recognize that community-based entrepreneurship can take other forms that may differ radically in almost every way from the model described above. Equally important is the fact that, while modern ideas of social entrepreneurship have only been around for the past few decades, the actual practice has existed for much longer. In their article "Economic Development, Entrepreneurial Embeddedness and Resilience: The Case of Pubs in Rural Ireland," Ignazio Cabras and Matthew Mount (2016) describe a system that fits many of the principles of social entrepreneurship, while neither they nor the people about whom they are writing use that term. This system has little in common with the standard view of social entrepreneurship outlined in the previous paragraph. The Irish pub system has existed for well over a hundred years, much longer than the concept of social entrepreneurship. Further, it was not created deliberately to benefit the community; in fact, it was not deliberately created at all. Rather it evolved in response to economic demand like any commercial enterprise and various community benefits became attached to it over time. The pub system is part of a developed western culture, demonstrating that, contrary to popular belief, such cultures are not always ill suited for social enterprises. This is particularly shown in the case of Ireland because the pub system evolved organically without external assistance which is not the case in many social enterprises.

Cabras and Mount collected data on pubs in rural Ireland with a particular focus on the challenges they face and how they are impacted by changes in the modern world, in Irish government and in economic policy as a whole. Data on the pubs were collected by sending pub owners a survey, either by mail or by email, that asked them about general statistics for the pub, typical profits and losses, source of the pubs' supplies, employment, and what issues the pub is facing. Pub contact information was obtained via access to the Vintners Federation of Ireland membership database. Unfortunately, this system of nonincentivized voluntary responses is not always effective at producing high compliance or ensuring a representational sample of data. In this case, only 16.5 percent of pubs contacted chose to complete the survey, which raises some questions about the representativeness of the data generated.

The data were also corroborated by ten detailed interviews with specific pub managers (Cabras & Mount, 2016: 258), lasting half an hour each and being recorded for later transcription. As the authors indicate, "The evidence gathered from the interviews is not intended as a 'representative' sample. Rather, the material is used to provide greater depth concerning points already raised in the context of the questionnaire," especially difficulties faced by pubs and what measures are being taken to address them (Cabras & Mount, 2016: 260). This still leaves the question of how typical the data really are, given the small sample size. The data is rendered more reliable by the fact that the 16.5 percent response rate did still include responses from all Irish counties and, in fact, was divided fairly evenly between counties, which is not typical for a voluntary response survey (Cabras & Mount, 2016: 261).

According to the data, there are currently about 7,400 pubs in operation in Ireland (Cabras & Mount, 2016: 255) almost 50 percent of which have been in operation since before 1913 (Cabras & Mount, 2016: 261). Pubs surveyed generated average revenue of 2,000 Euro a week, and as a whole, Irish pubs generate nearly five billion Euro a year from the sale of drinks alone, though, as will be discussed, they may provide other services as well. Clearly, pubs provide significant economic benefits to the communities in which they exist, but their value is social as well. As is the case in many social enterprises, "publicans appear to be at the center of many virtuous circles created between pubs and other small businesses operating within local supply chains. In such spatially reduced context, these individual businessmen may frequently have different occupations (e.g. auctioneers, part-time farmers and local politicians), with the most successful publicans running other businesses aside their pubs. In such circumstances, publicans may achieve a 'privileged' position with regard to facilitating and strengthening communal relationships among residents, by effectively shaping many of the economic and social dynamics occurring in rural and remote areas" (Cabras & Mount, 2016: 273).

On the most basic level, the pubs serve as important loci of interaction where people meet and socialize. In rural areas, they may be the primary form of social contact and vital to building community (Cabras & Mount, 2016: 257). Because they are the site of interpersonal interaction, pubs are also a significant means of facilitating business networking among community members. Pubs are also a forum for advertising locally produced goods and services and can even act as a kind of miniature market, allowing patrons to purchase these products on premise (Cabras & Mount, 2016: 255). In addition to providing a positive venue for socializing, pubs also serve as an important safety measure as they provide a public place for and, therefore a check on, alcohol consumption. As pub patronage has decreased, the incidence of alcohol related issues, such as traffic accidents and alcoholism, in Ireland has increased (Cabras & Mount, 2016: 272).

Pubs also provide their communities with the important economic assets of employment and training. In particular, pubs are the main providers of part-time employment and, thus, a valuable resource for women with children. In fact, pubs' busiest times are nights and weekends, and they prefer to hire additional workers on a part-time basis to cover these hours, providing the perfect option for part-time employment to people who need to care for children, attend school, or work another job during the day (Cabras & Mount, 2016: 269). This is equal opportunity employment, as at least half the pub workers are female. Three-quarters of pubs provide some form of employment in their community, with the average pub hiring three regular employees, one on a full-time and two on a part-time basis. Pubs also pay an average of 10.30 Euro per hour (Cabras & Mount, 2016: 263) which is an improvement on Ireland's minimum wage of 9.55 (Citizens Information, 2016). Pub work also provides training and work experience that can improve future employment or business opportunities. In particular, it serves to enhance "soft-skills such as customer service, time management, organization and leadership" (Cabras & Mount, 2016: 257). This benefits not only the employees but also the local economy as a whole since other businesses then have a pool of more skilled labor to draw upon (Cabras & Mont, 2016: 271).

The other major way in which pubs benefit their community is as consumers, who stimulate the local economy through purchasing supplies for their businesses. In fact, two-thirds of pubs do not make regular use of national chains for supplies. More specifically, in terms of purchasing supplies "The majority of respondents used large retailers either rarely or never (32 % and 43 % of responses, respectively) and did get supplies from specialized retailers for licensed businesses either often or always (19% and 51% of responses, respectively). The use of local retailers showed somewhat mixed results, with 30% of respondents using them on a regular basis and only 10% using them almost exclusively" (Cabras & Mount, 2016: 263). The authors speculate that the numbers for local support are not higher because of the number of pubs that primarily or exclusively serve alcohol, and Ireland possesses a limited number of locally based liquor suppliers. In addition, customers may desire name brand drinks that need to be purchased from national suppliers.

In light of the above information, it seems that pubs that serve meals in addition to drinks are the ones that provide the most benefit to the local community. These are the pubs that are the most likely to need additional employees to wait tables; so, they offer more jobs and training options to the community (Cabras & Mount, 2016: 266). Likewise, because of the issue with a lack of small alcohol suppliers indicated above, pubs serving food are significantly more likely to contribute to small businesses and local sellers, to the tune of about 600 Euro a month (Cabras & Mount, 2016: 270). Interestingly, the data also suggests pubs that serve food are also the most financially successful (Cabras & Mount, 2016: 263) indicating that this may be one of the virtuous cycles social entrepreneurship attempts to cultivate. However, only 25 percent of pubs opt to serve food, while two-thirds opt for the less profitable and beneficial route of offering drinks only (Cabras & Mount 2016: 261). For this reason, it might be worth exploring ways of incentivizing more pubs to start offering food for the benefit this would provide to everyone involved.

This is of special importance, as many pubs are experiencing financial difficulties. The data indicate that pubs frequently spend half or more of what they bring in just to cover their operating costs, and the situation is becoming worse as most pubs surveyed reported both a decrease in revenues and an increase in costs. One-third reported that costs had increased in the past year by 10 percent or more and that revenues in the same period had dropped by at least 25 percent (Cabras & Mount, 2016: 260). In addition, one thousand pubs were closed in the six years leading up to 2012, which also resulted in the loss of 12,500 jobs (Cabras & Mount, 2016: 255). This is concerning because the pub system is worth preserving both for its cultural relevance and because of the various economic and social benefits it bestows on the communities in which it operates.

The main difficulties facing pubs stem from aspects of the modern world bleeding into the rural communities where they operate, which frequently lack the resources or economic skills to respond promptly or properly. Many of these difficulties stem from laws passed by the county or national government, about which pub owners may have little or no say. On the most basic level, higher levels of taxation increase pub operating costs as do policies that increase "Licensing costs, associated with costs such as insurance and health and safety requirements" (Cabras & Mount, 2016: 268). Another concern involves policies regarding alcohol sales. Pubs are dependent on large chain suppliers for name brand alcohol; so, these brands are able to charge as much as they wish and the pubs lack the leverage to change this (Cabras & Mount, 2016: 268–269). The government not only allows this situation to exist but also permits these brands to sell their products much more cheaply to retail stores, creating a strong financial incentive for people to purchase their own alcohol rather than going to a pub (Cabras & Mount, 2016: 271). The government has made the situation worse by raising excise duties on alcohol, increasing the cost to pub owners by as much as 18 percent (Cabras & Mount, 2016: 272).

Another area in which modernization has affected pubs is in terms of lifestyle changes and health concerns. The government has responded to these trends by instituting a smoking ban and stricter drunk driving regulations, both of which reduce the business in pubs (Cabras & Mount, 2016: 268). As in the case of taxes and distribution costs, the government has not only failed to take action to lessen the impact on pub owners, but also, at times, has pursued policies that have made the situation worse for them. In particular, the government has failed to invest in a viable system of public transit. This has many wide-ranging consequences on community wellbeing beyond the scope of this discussion but, germane to this argument, deprives patrons of a way of getting safely home from the pub. In order to keep their customers, some pub owners have tried driving them home themselves or hiring drivers to do so, but here again, government policy regarding fees and liability renders this infeasible in many cases.

This lack of support from the government reflects no effort to figure out the needs of pubs or what policies would benefit them. Pub owners surveyed said they would appreciate being consulted by the government regarding policies that affect them, and it might prove beneficial to treat pubs "as business groups rather than individual businesses, discussing collective strategies/solutions that could work for pubs as well as for the areas they serve" (Cabras & Mount, 2016: 272–273).

There are also some challenges not directly related to government policies. For example, the increasing mobility of the modern world means many people now opt to move away from their local towns to seek employment in urban areas, especially the types of people who would have previously taken part-time jobs at the pub. This means not only that pubs are losing potential employees but also any employees they do have may then relocate, taking the experience and training they receive elsewhere; so, the community will no longer benefit from them (Cabras & Mount, 2016: 266).

Yet, despite the fact that conditions may look bleak for pubs, some signs indicate that they can be brought into the modern world in ways that will ultimately benefit both them and their communities. For one thing, in order to attract more customers and boost revenues, many pubs are making the decision to offer additional services, like serving food, as noted above (Cabras & Mount, 2016: 270). In addition, the government has opted to provide assistance in a small way, but one that has important implications for social entrepreneurship. In 2014, it passed a law allowing for the creation of a special transport system based on the rural hackney license. This allows individuals or small businesses to purchase a license to provide transportation for pay in their local area for a much lower cost than a standard transit license. This provides a way for individuals to run their own business, create more local wealth, assist both local residents and other businesses, including pubs, by enabling the people to access the goods and services they need. This creates a greater sense of community by allowing people in sparsely populated regions to gather together more easily (Cabras & Mount, 2016:

272–273). All of this offers hope that pubs can adapt to the modern world and continue to provide social and economic benefit to their communities.

It is important to note that social enterprises in native communities also experience difficulties integrating with the modern world and that financial success can present as much of a threat to social enterprises as financial difficulty. This is the situation facing the Ixtlan Group. Having obtained certification from the Forest Stewardship Council, the Ixtlan Group has started gaining international recognition, increasing sales of Ixtlan's forestry products. The increased profit has had numerous benefits. For one thing, it has allowed the Ixtlan Group to modernize its operations through the purchase of forestry technology, like a mechanized sawmill and greenhouse designed to maximize growth of new tree seedlings (Maguirre et al., 2016: 181–182).

Another benefit of financial success is the increased prosperity of the town of Ixtlan. Almost 100 percent of the buildings have plumbing and electricity, 20 percent more than in the rest of Mexico. Residents show a similar positive change in factors such as the ownership of cars and computers and an increase of 30 percent in access to social security (Maguirre et al., 2016: 182–183). This prosperity has attracted many people to Ixtlan from other regions as the working conditions and benefits are so much better than in other areas. Twenty percent of the employees in Ixtlan are now nonresidents. Businesses have also started to move in from other areas to tap into the increased affluence of Ixtlan (Maguirre et al., 2016: 184–185), which allows the residents access to many modern amenities not previously available. While this may seem positive on its surface, there is the definite risk of serious drawbacks in the long term. If the flow of workers from outside does not abate, they may soon come into competition with local residents for jobs. At that point, the Ixtlan Group's policy not to fire any workers may become a liability. Likewise, the influx of outside companies may take business away from local enterprises, undercutting one of the Ixtlan Group's most beneficial practices of assisting the local residents to generate their own wealth. Thus, without some form of intervention, Ixtlan's exceptional prosperity might prove its own undoing.

Just as Ixtlan's local prosperity is creating the seeds to undercut itself, Ixtlan Group's national and international success is a danger to social enterprise in a different way. In addition to the international trade mentioned above, "This social enterprise is helping other communities to replicate its business model so it can find partners to export fine furniture; it is also moving part of the production to other regions to improve quality; and it has developed informal partnerships with foreign suppliers to increase productivity" (Maguirre et al., 2016: 184–185). Again, this all seems positive at first glance. However, if the company is moving production to other regions and purchasing from outside suppliers, this may decrease the integration of company and community that was an important part of the Ixtlan Group's role as a social enterprise.

However, there is another even more serious issue that has arisen from the new international focus of the Ixtlan Group, an issue that represents an Achilles heel of social enterprises (Maguirre et al., 2016: 185):

> There are managers within the organization that want to prioritize the economic dimension, arguing that without organic growth and additional resources, the social and environmental dimensions cannot be addressed. They also remark that Ixtlan is competing with commercial entities that do not bear the costs of a social entity, since most commercial entities do not even comply with mandatory benefits for their labor in that region. However, some workers believe that philosophy will betray Ixtlan's purpose, compromising some of the empowerment mechanisms the organization has created. This struggle (and market pressures) may originate the replacement or modification of some of these mechanisms in the near future, demanding further social innovation to generate wellbeing in the community and the region.

The defining feature of social enterprises is the combination of profit and social benefit and, for the social enterprise to function properly, one can not be neglected in order to benefit the other. It is not simply a concern that if an organization like the Ixtlan Group sacrifices social benefit for the sake of profit, it will no longer fit the criteria of a social enterprise. The philosophy of social enterprise, as has been demonstrated in this chapter, is based on the idea of the virtuous cycle, where the financial and social aspects of the venture reinforce one another and are stronger and more successful together than either would be alone. Central to the idea of social enterprise is the notion that the conventional wisdom of focus on profit above all else is incorrect, not just from a moral perspective, but from a financial one. This may, in fact, point to one of the main weaknesses of social enterprises based in communities of native peoples, as they may not need to contend with this belief at first and so may be vulnerable when success brings them into contact with other businesses with more traditional approaches.

The important points to understand here are that social enterprises can take many forms, ancient and recent, planned and organic, involving native and developed communities. But in all cases, social enterprises do not exist in a vacuum. At some point, they will need to contend with the outside world and the common focus on profit, which will present challenges to the enterprise whether it experiences success or hardship. While the approaches needed in each of these cases will vary, and indeed all social enterprises are unique and will need somewhat different strategies, the basic need to create and maintain a virtuous cycle between profit and social benefit remains constant. The fact also remains that many different types of communities from all over the world can benefit from the implementation and maintenance of such cycles.

References

Cabras, I., & Mount, M. (2016). Economic development, entrepreneurial embeddedness and resilience: the case of pubs in rural Ireland. *European Planning Studies* 24 (2): 254–276.

Maguirre, M., Ruelas, G., & De La Torre, C. (2016). Women empowerment through social innovation in indigenous social enterprises. *Revista de Administração Mackenzie* 17 (6): 164–190.

Chapter 10
Social Entrepreneurship among Native Peoples of the Americas: A Model or an Exception?

One of the great advantages of social entrepreneurship is its flexibility and ability to be used to beneficial effect in a wide variety of communities. It has been used as a tool to address various economic and social problems among the Native peoples of the Americas. This chapter explores two specific incidences of this use, one an individual effort by a single reservation community in the continental United States undertaken recently and the other a statewide government policy for addressing the needs of Native peoples in Alaska, which has been in operation since 1971. Although these ventures have provided benefits to the communities in question, as well as valuable insights regarding the various advantages and challenges of different forms of social entrepreneurship, they do not seem to be regarded as useful models for implementing social entrepreneurship in other communities. This is apparently because the community-based aspects of social entrepreneurship are seen as appropriate for Native peoples due to their perceived philosophy of interdependency but not for mainstream American society, with its more individualistic bent. However, the principles of social entrepreneurship can be used to positive effect in many different situations including, perhaps especially, in the developed world, so it is worth looking at these examples from Arizona and Alaska.

It is no surprise that Native Americans in the continental United States would experience economic, community, and other issues, perhaps in part because the myriad issues faced by these communities and fostered by the reservation system are so interconnected, creating a circular effect that builds on itself. As a simplified example, poor economic performance may lead to low self-esteem, which may lead to substance abuse, which may in turn lead to more poor economic performance. Further, as such trends spread and become more pervasive in a community, they may become more complicated, more deeply entrenched, and more difficult to address. In their 2016 article, "Entrepreneurship Education: A Strength-Based Approach to Substance Use and Suicide Prevention for American Indian Adolescents," Lauren Tingey, Francene Larzelere-Hinton, Novalene Goklish, Allison Ingalls, Todd Craft, Feather Sprengeler, Courtney McGuire, and Allison Barlow describe an attempt to better conditions in a single Native American community by targeting the specific problems of substance abuse and suicide. Members of the White Mountain Apache Tribe populate the Fort Apache Indian reservation in Arizona and are subjects of this work. The chosen method

DOI 10.1515/9781547400461-010

of intervention is an entrepreneurship training program, which the designers believe has the potential to not only address the specific target issues, but also to start a chain reaction that will expand outward to address other related issues in the community.

Economic conditions on the Fort Apache reservation are certainly not ideal. Over 60 percent of the population is not gainfully employed, with at least as many living below the poverty line (Tingey et al., 2016: 253). Due to a number of factors, including the physical isolation of the reservation, employment options are highly limited, consisting in large measure of the reservation stereotypes of museum, casino, and ski resort jobs, though the tribe does produce some goods through lumber and agriculture. There are also a few more community-focused sources of employment such as health services, schools, social services, and the local branch of Johns Hopkins University with a focus on the institution's Center for Indian Health (Tingey et al., 2016: 252). There is also some history of entrepreneurship in the community via the existence of the tailgate market, a daily outdoor gathering where small businesses or individuals can congregate to offer locally produced goods and services that are difficult to procure from the outside world due to the reservation's isolated location, with an emphasis on traditional crafts (Tingey et al., 2016: 254). Still, endeavors such as this have only managed to have a limited impact on local conditions.

In addition to being a problem in its own right, the economic depression in the community has led to the spread of other social and personal problems. In particular, the poor economic conditions have fostered a feeling of helplessness and of lacking the ability to take action to better one's situation, frequently triggering hopelessness and depression, which many of the residents attempt to cope with via alcohol and substance abuse, with some becoming suicidal. This trend is particularly prevalent among the young people, who view themselves as having no future and being powerless to create one. Given that 54 percent of the population is under the age of twenty-five, these issues are very prominent in the community (Tingey et al., 2016: 253). In an unfortunate irony, the feelings of being powerless to change their lot, have led many of the young people to lose any sense of commitment to education, one of the things that might actually help to put them in a better economic situation. Students perform below the national average in reading and math, with only 40 percent of third graders rated as proficient. The percentage of those who manage to graduate high school is virtually the same at 41 percent (Tingey et al., 2016: 253). Thus, the youth of the community provide an ideal entry point for addressing socioeconomic concerns of reservation life, as they represent both the largest and most vulnerable group in the community, the hope being that improvements for this significant group would create a ripple effect to improve the community at large.

The fact that targeting youth issues is meant to be a community-wide process, and a means for facilitating general improvement, was made clear from the beginning. The stated goal is: "to develop prevention models targeting key determinants of mental health and well-being at the level of whole communities situated within their larger socioeconomic contexts... Researchers urge for new initiatives that examine societal-level factors such as poverty and unemployment, and make an explicit commitment to local capacity building and community health, with an overarching emphasis on resilience" (Tingey et al., 2016: 248).

This, of course, begs the question of what is resilience and how does it relate to community building and improved socioeconomic conditions. The authors define resilience as being based on three factors: connection to other individuals in the community, connection to community institutions, and connection to self, in the form of self-esteem and optimism (Tingey et al., 2016: 249). While these represent a strategy more than a definition, they attempt to actualize the strategy in several ways. In terms of the youth group, the first refers to fostering connections to adults in the community who can make the youth feel cared about, act as mentor figures, watch for signs of substance abuse, and intervene if they are detected (Tingey et al., 2016: 249–50). Connectedness to community institutions for youth means encouraging them to stay in school. This ensures that they will be surrounded by supportive peers and adults and will have the means to improve their skills and employability for the future (Tingey et al., 2016: 250). The final part of the triad involves feeling confidence in oneself and believing one has the ability to have an impact on one's own life.

These three components are interconnected in important ways especially in regards to preventing suicide and substance abuse. Having caring figures in one's life raises one's emotional state, as does being part of a community, such as a school. Likewise both individuals and groups can watch for the signs of self-destructive behavior and provide positive interventions. In addition, both mentor figures and educational institutions can provide youth with directional guidance for the future as well as skill building that will be useful down the road. This provides a greater sense of control that leads to higher self-esteem and less likelihood of resorting to destructive behaviors. In other words, "A positive youth development framework posits that youth who develop mastery and are supported by caring adults and peers to cultivate new skills are more likely to exercise control over their lives by making healthy choices and withstanding external pressures" (Tingey et al., 2016: 251). The ideal for true resilience is to simultaneously improve people's economic conditions and mental and emotional conditions to create a virtuous cycle. Improved self-esteem contributes to greater motivation and accomplishment in the physical realm while improved physical circumstances simultaneously provide the basis for a more solid emotional foundation.

The White Mountain Apache Tribe, in partnership with the Johns Hopkins University Center for American Indian Health, decided on the model of entrepreneurship education as the best method to address this complex issue and try to create the virtuous cycle described above. Tingey et al. define entrepreneurship education as "the pursuit of opportunity beyond the resources currently controlled... Entrepreneurship education increases motivation for under-resourced groups to complete formal education, promotes vocational and social skills, and enables youth to contribute to their community's economic development" (Tingey et al., 2016: 251). This clearly articulates the benefits of such a program, not only to those receiving the training but also to the community as a whole. The community will not only benefit from having mentally and emotionally stable youth and from future jobs generated by their entrepreneurial endeavors, but, because the program was established and is operated by community members, simply conducting the program serves as an important source of employment and community building (Tingey et al., 2016: 255).

The program created was known as the Arrowhead Business Group Apache Youth Entrepreneurship Program (ABG). It is a "16-lesson curriculum taught via discussion, games, hands-on learning, and multimedia. Approximately 60 hours of training over an 8-month period focus on entrepreneurship and business development, life skills, self-efficacy, and finance. Basic math computation skills and literacy are reinforced by training. ABG has varying instructional levels to address literacy challenges and either delayed or advanced academic skills" (Tingey et al., 2016: 255). Participants in the initial version of the program came from a randomly selected set of local youth, ages 13–16. Of the selected youth, two-thirds participated in the entrepreneurship-training program while one-third served as the control to test the effects of the program. Both groups participated in recreational activities provided by the program to rule out the possibility that the activity, alone, was critical (Tingey et al., 2016: 257). The efficacy of the program was assessed by means of an audio computer assisted self-interview program to ensure anonymity while simultaneously making the process easier for those with poor literacy skills. These computer-based interviews were conducted six months, one year, and two years after the program, and youth were given gift cards as an incentive to participate in the interviews. During the interviews, participants were asked to report on topics such as the degree of hope and control they felt in their life, their engagement in risk taking behavior, and their performance and motivation at school (Tingey et al., 2016: 258).

The original design for the program involved sixteen lessons. The first ten were taught at a summer camp and covered topics including setting goals, developing communication skills, resume building, budgeting, identifying community needs for specific products or services, branding, and drawing up a business plan. The program then continued during the school year and involved participants working in groups to design their own business over the course of six workshops (Tingey et al., 2016: 255–256). According to the program designers, "Youth practice public presentations and social networking skills. They map community assets with a focus on gaps in the local economy and identify opportunities for new businesses. Youth conduct market research and learn branding, marketing, and basic accounting concepts, which are then applied to a hands-on community-based selling event" (Tingey et al., 2016: 255). In addition to presenting what they had learned at the community event, participants could apply to receive funding for their business plan and receive mentoring from community members in order to bring the plan to fruition (Tingey et al., 2016: 255), providing an immediate tangible way for the program to bring more vitality to the reservation economy.

Based on the feedback from the pilot program, a few modifications were made. The summer camp was extended from three to five days and moved from an off-site location onto reservation land to better emphasize the connection between the skills taught and the community. The workshops were also restructured to make them more flexible and a better fit for participants' individual needs. This included scheduling—allowing the workshops to be held after school, during evenings, or weekends, depending on the other activities of the participants—as well as moving all the basic lessons to the summer camp so the workshops could be devoted to developing the groups' business plans (Tingey et al., 2016: 261–262).

In terms of the EST and RISE models described in Chapter 3, the program has both pros and cons. On the plus side, it acknowledges the importance of, and trains in, both hard and soft skills and includes a focus on individual skill building, like self-confidence and networking, rather than solely on generating a business plan. The fact that the program focuses on fostering basic understanding of skills, rather than climbing the RISE ladder to mastery, should not be considered a major weakness considering that the program is targeted at young teens/high school students. The two main downsides of the program, which are intertwined, are the lack of clear evaluation methods for skill development and a heavy focus on starting rather than running a business. The article does not mention any method used by the program to evaluate participant's competencies in individual entrepreneurial skills. The program culminates in a single event, a selling day where participants unveil their new business plans and take them for a test drive, together with a contest to choose a business plan to receive funding for ongoing operation after the close of the program. The difficulty here is that the above activities view the end product as a whole, whether the participant was able to produce a successful business plan or not, and do not provide the feedback regarding strengths and weaknesses of individual entrepreneurial skills which is central to the RISE method. The other issue is that the program focuses more on "traditional" entrepreneurial skills to plan and start a business, like budgeting, assessing a market need, etc., rather than skills designed to sustain a business long term; even the interpersonal skills covered are geared toward self-confidence and networking but do not support skill sets like ongoing problem solving or motivating and managing employees (Lyons & Lyons, 2015).

The program diverges from many other entrepreneurship training efforts in ways that tie it more closely to social entrepreneurship. For one thing, there is a strong focus on life skill building and community interaction. Another factor involves a commitment to promoting respect for Native American tribal values as well as gender equality both through the content of the lessons and in the selection of teachers, who are respected members of the reservation community and are arranged in pairs, one man and one woman for each lesson (Tingey et al., 2016: 255, 260, 261).

However, there is also a downside to this in that outsiders, including Tingey and the other authors of the article, do not recognize that the White Mountain Apache Tribe is participating in a wider institution of social entrepreneurship. While social entrepreneurship is certainly not a one-size-fits-all model, and the case of the West Side Xcelerator (see Chapter 6) is a testament to the dangers of not tailoring things closely enough to the needs of the individual community, it is important to recognize that social entrepreneurship is a system that can be adjusted in various ways to support a variety of social and economic structures. However, there is a danger, as in the case of the Westside Xcelerator, of viewing certain social structures as being "too individualistic" and therefore not suited to this type of intervention. As Tingey et al. point out "we adapted conventional entrepreneurial concepts for the Apache cultural context. Many existing youth entrepreneurship models we explored valued an individual approach to business development. However, in the participating and other AI communities, a collective approach is more appropriate. Thus, the ABG curriculum was designed to promote a cooperative methodology to entrepreneurship and to teach youth how the entire community benefits from business creation" (Tingey et al., 2016: 260). This shows that, instead, the emphasis on community building is viewed as being an unusual exception, which needed to be included to accommodate Native American social values rather than something that has wider applicability on a world-wide scale. This trend can also be seen in other examples of social entrepreneurship among the Native peoples of the Americas, such as the case of the Alaska Native Corporations (ANCs) described later in this chapter and the Ixtlan group presented in the next chapter, which, while they may be different in form, are similar in philosophy to the developments in the White Mountain Apache tribe.

Considering the issues faced by the reservation system in the continental United States which can, at best, be addressed in piecemeal fashion through individual efforts like the entrepreneurial training program described above, it is not surprising that the state of Alaska would pursue alternative methods for addressing the situation of Native peoples within its borders. The approach decided on in the Alaskan Native Claims Settlement Act of 1971 was, at the time, a unique way of addressing the issue and remains a distinctive solution to this day. Each tribe or village was given the legal status of a corporation, with all residents as joint shareholders. This institution, ANC, was provided with land and funding by the government with the understanding that they would use these resources to start business ventures that would provide for their members in the future (Vazquez, 2016: 359). The article "A Business Entity by any Other Name: Corporation, Community, and Kinship" by Christian Vazquez explores in detail the various advantages and challenges of this system as well as how it compares to the B Corp, one type of benefit corporation, which is a more recent form of corporation enabling a focus on social goals in preference to, but not always to the exclusion of, profit available to the general public. However, not all states have enacted legislation for benefit corporations and the rules for incorporating vary from state to state; so, while it would be possible for Alaskan natives to enroll in a benefit corporation out of state, given the specific legal nature of the ANCs this could be highly impractical or impossible and the benefit corporation laws in other states might not be conducive to their specific needs, as will be explored below.

ANCs are very important economically to the state of Alaska, making up a quarter of Alaska's gross domestic product (GDP) and providing nearly 70 percent of Alaskan jobs (Vazquez, 2016: 360, 370). They are also the primary, often sole, means of providing for the needs of the Native people on many more levels than simply the financial. "Unlike traditional corporations, ANCs are not focused on boosting share prices or raising dividends. To be sure, all ANCs confer dividends to enrolled Alaska Natives. However, ANCs also supply shareholders with other nonconventional benefits such as scholarships, funeral benefits, charitable and in-kind donations, employment opportunities, cultural preservation, land management, opportunities for economic development and advocacy" (Vazquez, 2016: 367). Profit from the companies is often spent to improve the lives of the members in a variety of ways by funding "housing authorities, health organizations, or vocational schools... cultural preservation, land management, economic development, and issue advocacy. ANCs may also engage in preferential hiring for shareholders, which may take the form of employment, training, or internships" (Vazquez, 2016: 369).

In addition, "One of the most unique benefits that ANCs confer on shareholders is the manner in which they serve as advocates for Alaska Natives. Economies of scale permit ANCs to lobby and access legal expertise not otherwise possible for smaller villages or individual Alaska Natives" (Vazquez, 2016: 370). For example, the influence of the ANCs has played a significant role in the election, to both state offices and the national congress, of candidates with policies more friendly to Native people (Vazquez, 2016: 371).

All of this demonstrates that ANCs are true examples of social entrepreneurship as, not only do they use profits to provide benefits to the community, such as housing and education, but they also provide their members with training and skill building to increase their future autonomy and self-efficacy. In addition, they serve as a political base to advocate toward greater equality. However, despite the enormous potential of the ANCs on the social front as well as their very real economic impact, there are still concerns that the companies are not doing as much as they should to improve the wellbeing of the Native people.

One of the main challenges faced by the ANCs is that their members were not provided with instruction on how to conduct business or run a corporation and, as a consequence, encountered difficulty in generating the needed funds. While this trend has corrected itself somewhat over time (Vazquez, 2016: 360) it still remains a concern that "ANCs are a reversal of the traditional process of incorporation wherein a group finds an economic opportunity and organizes itself to exploit and capitalize on that opportunity. ANCs are again peculiar because a source other than their owners provided capital. Moreover, ANCs, unlike most corporations, did not begin with a business plan or product; instead they were funded first and then urged to create or find economic opportunities afterwards" (Vazquez, 2016: 356).

Another issue facing ANCs involves the complications involving the handling of company stock. In order to ensure that the ANCs remain focused on providing benefits to the Native people and do not evolve into standard, for-profit companies, members are forbidden from selling or trading their stock shares. At the time the ANCs were formed in 1971, all adult members of native tribes or groups were issued one hundred shares of stock in the ANC associated with their tribe or region. The problem arises in the fact that the number of stock shares issued at that time was absolute and finite which, combined with the prohibition on stock trading, means there is no way to provide stock to members of Native groups born after 1971(Vazquez, 2016: 359–360).

In order to address these and any other issues facing the ANCs, the state of Alaska reviews the ANC statutes and amends them as needed or extends previously granted exceptions and amendments. Important amendments involve relieving the ANCs of various restrictions and requirements of traditional for-profit corporations to help ease their transition into the business world, including exemption from certain taxes and federal security compliance and reporting rules, though they are still required to comply with state restrictions (Vazquez, 2016: 360, 364–366). Other revisions involve allowing ANC boards to create by-laws allowing members to pass stock onto their children (Vazquez, 2016: 360). These types of adjustments have done much to compensate for the deficiencies in the original ANC plan and "ANCs are generally given more discretion to manage themselves than other corporations. This accounts for their substantial exemption from federal regulation and the manner in which they largely self-regulate in accordance with Alaska's securities laws. This is so because, unlike other corporations, the shares in ANCs are nontransferable, tying ownership to a community with goals that transcend profit maximization. Overall, the primary purpose of ANCs is to raise the standard of living for Alaska Natives" (Vazquez, 2016: 367). However, as the ANCs grow and become more economically viable, their dedication and ability to perform their original purpose is called increasingly into question, due to fears that they will become more focused on profit than on continuing to provide benefits to Native people. This trend can be seen in the fact that, as the companies grow, the percentage, now over fifty, of non-native employees also grows while, at the same time, natives who desire employment with the ANCs are not always able to obtain it (Vazquez, 2016: 370).

In response to the above concerns, Vazquez's article explores the possibility of replacing the ANCs with B corporations, a type of socially focused entity available in other states regardless of ethnicity. In other words, "In states authorizing the B Corp form, these corporations may deviate from the profit maximization framework rooted in the concept of shareholder primacy and instead pursue the public benefit of society" (Vazquez, 2016: 372). The argument in favor of B Corps is that, as this approach is not based around a kinship model, it would eliminate any remaining issues regarding stockholders passing shares on to their children. It would also make the corporations subject to more accountability, which would make it easier to keep them on track in terms of their original goal of protecting native interests, while at the same time, maintaining their nonprofit status and keeping them free of many of the restrictions on for-profit companies (Vazquez, 2016: 373).

Unfortunately, the very things that make the idea of transitioning to a B Corp structure advantageous, also introduce new complications. While it might benefit ANC members to be able to transfer stock more freely inside their kinship groups, amendments to the original ANC rules have provided achievable, if cumbersome methods of doing this. Furthermore, it would definitely not be to the advantage of the Native people if company stock began to be traded to outsiders, especially in significant numbers. In fact, this would probably be the fastest way, despite the greater accountability rules, to cause the corporations to veer toward profit and away from a focus on the needs of the Native people. Thus, despite certain gains, removing the restrictions on stock trading would be a net disadvantage.

In addition, the increase in reporting requirements, despite the greater accountability it would provide, would, in and of itself, prove counter to the purpose of the ANCs. This is because B Corps are required to be overseen by an external certifying entity, in this case, an organization called B Lab. Therefore, "an ANC choosing to convert would have needed to rely on a third party likely ill-informed of the particular issues facing Alaska Natives. The reliance on the third party would remove the semiautonomy that ANCs have given Alaska Natives over their own affairs since the ANCSA settlement" (Vazquez, 2016: 374). In addition to the fact that the corporations would need to share the power of the board with an external entity in the form of a benefits director, the need to report to B Lab yearly or twice a year could have other consequences. For one thing, the actual process of collecting data and filing such a report carries a cost, not just financially, but in terms of expenditure of time and resources, which would divert resources that could be better used to support the company members, and would be especially costly for the smaller corporations (Vazquez, 2016: 374). In addition, the purpose of these reports is to ensure the company is continuing to fulfill its mission, in this case, to provide benefits to Alaskan Natives. While this seems like a good thing as it creates needed accountability, it also means that the corporations would be liable to sanction from B Lab, if they are not providing the agreed on benefits. This would be likely to induce companies to favor short-term sustainability over more experimental or risky ventures that might result in long-term gain (Vazquez, 2016: 377).

Besides the difficulties involved in the actual reporting process, there is also the fact that B Lab appoints a director to make sure that the company is acting in accordance with its mission and to oversee the reporting process. However, ANCs are usually operated by a board of elected officials, which spreads out power and provides the possibility of replacement if needed. Therefore, being required to have a single individual to fill such an influential role is contrary to the existing management structure of the companies and could have a variety of negative consequences, especially given the fact that B lab may be unfamiliar with the specific needs of the native groups (Vazquez, 2016: 376).

In addition, "Difficulties with quantifying less tangible benefits like employment training and cultural opportunities threaten to render the reports altogether useless. Third parties generating these reports, such as B Lab, would likely lack the cultural insights and understanding of Alaska Natives' interests necessary to draw meaningful conclusions. As a result, the B Corp form could have forced directors to rely upon metrics with faulty methodology to make their determinations to the detriment of the true interests most important to the Native community. Many of these interests, especially those that are not easily quantifiable such as the provision of particular vocational training in certain villages would suffer as a result" (Vazquez, 2016: 374–375). For all of the above reasons, despite the various issues with the current system of ANCs, Vazquez advises against a move to a B Corp format.

However, while Vazquez is probably correct in the assessment that the ANCs would ultimately not benefit from transitioning into B Corps, there are wider implications to consider in terms of the role social entrepreneurship can or should play in the world at large. It is probably also true that the community needs of Alaskan Natives differ from those of, say, an inner city community, and that it would be more difficult to find business experts, like B Lab, who would understand those specific needs. In some ways, it is accurate to say, "ANCs have managed to aggregate talent and capital for the Native people of Alaska. This has been accomplished by tailoring the needs of the corporate form toward those of Alaska Natives over the course of the last forty-five years. The subsequent entities that have developed from continuous Congressional adjustments to ANCSA are distinct from comparable corporations, with such deviations needed to bridge the gap between corporation, community, and kinship" (Vazquez, 2016: 371). On the other hand, it seems unwise to take the view that only Native people want, need, or are capable of "bridging the gap between corporation, community and kinship." While they may approach these things in slightly different ways, so may other community groups and, as other chapters in this book point out, many types of people and communities can benefit from social entrepreneurship, and the more that do so the greater the net benefit overall.

This is of particular importance when the two case studies in this chapter are taken together, as both seem to make this assumption that combining business and community is a thing special and unique to Native people because of their particular culture and values. It is important to remember, as Lyons expresses in "Leveraging Commercial and Social Entrepreneurship for the Revitalization of Marginalized Urban Communities," that the principles of social entrepreneurship can be adapted to a wide variety of situations, including cultures that are commonly viewed as individualistic as opposed to communally oriented. He warns against the dangers of getting trapped into an either/or mindset where "We can choose either free markets *or* socialism. We must serve either shareholders *or* stakeholders. We can serve the interests of the few *or* the many... Why can't we use markets to solve social problems? What prevents us from serving shareholders *and* stakeholders (doing well *and* good) at the same time?... The ultimate manifestation of the 'sweet spot' where the market meets social responsibility is the work of social entrepreneurs, who employ the mindset, skills, tools, techniques and processes of commercial entrepreneurship in pursuit of a social mission. Whether they structure their social enterprises as nonprofits, for-profits or hybrids of the two, social entrepreneurs hold the key" (Lyons, 2016: 2–3). For this reason, the experiences of the ANCs and the training program at the White Mountain Apache reservation may still have valuable information to provide about what does and does not work that could be applied, perhaps with slight modification, to other social ventures and, as such, deserve to be considered in detail as more than mere cultural artifacts.

References

Kickul, J., & Lyons, T.S. (2016). *Understanding social entrepreneurship: The relentless pursuit of mission in an ever changing world*, Second edition. New York: Routledge.

Lyons, T., & Lyons, J. (2015). A skills assessment approach for operationalizing entrepreneur skill theory. White Paper. Morristown, NJ: LEAP, LLC.

Lyons, T. (2016). Leveraging commercial and social entrepreneurship for the revitalization of marginalized urban communities. Activating Markets for Social Change Conference, Sol Price Center for Social Innovation, University of Southern California, April 14–16.

Tingey, L., Larzelere-Hinton, F., Goklish, N., Ingalls, A., Craft, T., Sprengeler, F., McGuire, C., & Barlow, A. (2016). Entrepreneurship education: A strength-based approach to substance use and suicide prevention for American Indian adolescents. *American Indian & Alaska Native Mental Health Research: The Journal of the National Center* 23 (3): 248–270.

Vazquez, C. (2016). A business entity by any other name: Corporation, community, and kinship. *Alaska Law Review* 33 (2): 353–358.

Chapter 11
Necessary but Not Sufficient:
Only Systemic Approaches Transform

Wealth inequality has put a strain on economies and societies around the world.[1] We are only just beginning to feel its true impact. If left to fester, it will ultimately threaten the economic wellbeing of millions, if not billions, of people. It will undermine democratic institutions. It could lead to increased divisive behavior and resulting conflict. It likely will lead to increased isolation at a time when, more than ever, people around the world need to be working together on systemic solutions to "wicked" problems.

There is no panacea for wealth inequality, but it is possible to make wealth building an opportunity that is more widely available. As we have argued throughout the book, this can be achieved by fostering entrepreneurship. The goal of entrepreneurship is to create wealth through innovation and growth. Successful entrepreneurship contributes directly to the benefit of the entrepreneur and her or his family by creating a business asset, but it can also benefit the community and society as a whole. It does so by bringing new and better ways of doing things to the markets that need them; by creating jobs; by generating income, which when saved and invested becomes wealth; and by creating dollars for investment back into the infrastructures, hard and soft, that contribute to wellbeing and continued innovation and growth. In this way, it can both initiate and perpetuate a virtuous cycle.

If we resist the temptation to treat entrepreneurship as an elitist activity that can only be carried out by people who are born to the task—who have the necessary innate traits—we begin to understand that entrepreneurship is a way of thinking and acting that can be learned and applied by anyone who is properly motivated (Neck et al., 2018; Lichtenstein & Lyons, 2010). This opens the door to taking a developmental approach to fostering it. Rather than being reduced to "picking winners" or trying to predict (with historically very limited accuracy) who the next successful entrepreneur will be and the industry in which they will

---

[1] Portions of this chapter are excerpted with the permission of the Sol Price Center for Social Innovation from Lyons, T.S. (2016). "Leveraging Commercial and Social Entrepreneurship for the Revitalization of Marginalized Urban Communities," Framing Paper for the Panel on Social Entrepreneurship, *Activating Markets for Social Change Conference*, Los Angeles, CA: Sol Price Center for Social Innovation, Price School of Public Policy, University of Southern California (April 15).

DOI 10.1515/9781547400461-011

operate, we will have positioned ourselves to expand entrepreneurship's reach by creating an environment that supports the success of anyone and everyone who chooses to participate. Those who choose not to participate can still benefit from increased entrepreneurial activity in the community-developing ways described above.

Implementing this strategy requires a different perspective on how we develop our communities. Let us consider the old environmentalist bromide, "Think globally and act locally." What does it actually mean? It is calling for a blended perspective that acknowledges both the opportunities inherent in thinking about the ways in which each community connects to others throughout the world and the reality that local context is important when it comes to addressing the needs of the residents of the given community. In many ways, it reflects the kind of thinking that was *not* part of the globalization of the U.S. economy that has taken place over the past several decades. In our rush to capture the economic opportunities afforded by globalization, its uneven impacts on this country's communities were ignored. While some flourished, creating a wealthy elite class, others withered, leaving behind an economically marginalized population. Wealth inequality grew.

The recent reaction to this situation has been the opposite extreme. Communities, and the entire country, are trying to wall themselves off from the rest of the world, taking the misguided view that this will reverse the situation. History tells us that it will likely have the opposite effect. Instead, we should be taking the original prescription to heart. If we think strategically about how we can link our communities to the opportunities afforded by the global economy while, at the same time, ensuring that the way in which we pursue these opportunities is attuned to the needs of the individual community by driving these efforts from the community level, we can achieve the balance prescribed and mitigate wealth inequality. This can be accomplished when an entire community is thinking and acting entrepreneurially—what some have called civic entrepreneurship. In many communities, this will require the courage and commitment to make a culture change, however (Macke, 2018). We will need to move these communities from a culture of dependency to one of independence and openness to change.

In addition, we need to stop pursuing growth at the expense of development. There is nothing inherently "bad" about growth, but it is merely more of something. What we really want for our communities is "better." We want to transform our economies to ensure a better quality of life. We want a blend of development and growth—more of better. When applied to entrepreneurship, we are not merely seeking more entrepreneurs; we want more high quality (economically successful) entrepreneurs.

This brings us back to the idea of taking a "developmental" approach to fostering entrepreneurship. It has been pointed out elsewhere that the best measure of an entrepreneur's quality is her or his skill level (Lichtenstein & Lyons, 2010). If we want to improve that entrepreneur's quality, we must focus on developing their skills. This requires jettisoning the old focus on business development and putting the spotlight squarely on the entrepreneur. If entrepreneurs are to be successful at wealth building through the creation of a business asset, they need the requisite skills. These skills will allow *them* to be the business developers, understanding the other resources they require for success and where and how to find them. In this way, we increase their capacity to build wealth.

Making the entrepreneur the centerpiece of enterprise development efforts anchors them firmly in the local context. Developing entrepreneurs by building their skills empowers them to engage effectively with the global economy to generate wealth, thereby linking the local and the global in a more constructive way. Doing this in an inclusive manner spreads the opportunity to build wealth more broadly than it is currently distributed.

It would be tempting to label this an "everybody's an entrepreneur" approach. While we want to support the activities of as many motivated entrepreneurs as possible, how we define "entrepreneurship" remains important. What qualifies as entrepreneurship must be capable of creating wealth. As we emphasized in Chapter 4, wealth is only created through activities that involve innovation and a goal of growth. A true wealth-building entrepreneur must find a way to take something that is new to a market that needs it and be able to scale that activity.

Thus, a strategy for broadly building wealth through entrepreneurship must support the efforts of actual wealth-creating entrepreneurs and do so in a way that is inclusive of all who choose to participate, and it must do this in a manner that is respectful of local culture but effectively connects local entrepreneurs to the opportunities afforded by the global economy. This is a noble aspiration, but how do we make it a reality? We now look back at our case studies to see how they can inform us, individually and collectively, and how these lessons can serve as a springboard into the future.

Lessons Learned from Individual Case Studies

In this book, we have shared eight examples of efforts by very different communities to encourage entrepreneurship as a means to wealth creation and constructive community development. Some were very successful, while others failed. Some represent pilot efforts that await full implementation. Individually and collectively, they provide lessons in what works in such endeavors and what does not as well as why.

The example of Competition THRIVE, discussed in Chapter 5, involves the collaboration of a city government, a private foundation and a university. This intersectoral partnership was crucial to the success of this effort to effectively support entrepreneurship in immigrant communities of New York City. This example fully reflects the work of social entrepreneurs to foster commercial entrepreneurship that was advocated in Chapter 4. With the financial support of the foundation and the technical support of the university, the city encouraged innovation among social entrepreneurs, entrepreneurship support organizations (ESOs) with the mission to improve the economies of immigrant neighborhoods through entrepreneurship, to allow them to better serve their client entrepreneurs. In this way, these immigrant entrepreneurs could more successfully build wealth. This case shows one way that markets can be used responsibly to address wealth inequality and transform people's lives.

In Chapter 6, the Westside Xcelerator is examined. While this effort was technically a failure, this was not due to the quality of the idea. This program sought to encourage business growth by minority entrepreneurs, a group that historically operates "mom and pop" necessity businesses that serve local markets. Through a combination of financial investment, coaching and connecting to markets outside the community, the Westside Xcelerator encouraged its client entrepreneurs to engage with the larger economy and positioned them to build wealth. The program's downfall was caused by the overwhelming nonentrepreneurship challenges that face urban minority groups and its inability to effectively integrate its strategy into serving the broader needs of the community. It is an object lesson in the importance of accounting for and addressing local context in any effort to encourage entrepreneurship.

The Michigan State University (MSU) Product Center (Chapter 7) carries out a statewide program to encourage entrepreneurship in the agri-food sector of the Michigan economy. While its industry scope is narrow, the Product Center is inclusive in the entrepreneurial population it serves. It is also holistic in its approach, using partnerships and networks, both inside and outside MSU, to create an ecosystem of support for its client entrepreneurs.

Another intersectoral partnership lies at the heart of the Warsaw Entrepreneurship Forum in Poland, discussed in Chapter 8. The social entrepreneurs in this case are the Municipality of Warsaw and Kozminski University. They sought to create entrepreneur networks in the city by district to encourage social capital building by entrepreneurs and improve the working relationship between the local government and its resident entrepreneurs—another case of social entrepreneurs fostering commercial entrepreneurship for the benefit of the community.

Despite the temptation to focus exclusively on high technology entrepreneurs, the principals in this case kept the program inclusive.

Chapter 9 addresses two cases of entrepreneurship that benefits its community. In the case of the lumber enterprise in Ixtlan, Mexico, we have a social enterprise with a mission of improving the lives of community residents by using its earned income to provide multiple kinds of support. Among these is the fostering of new businesses through low-cost loans, empowerment efforts, and management training. While this support of commercial entrepreneurship is exclusively for community residents, it is inclusive in the sense that women can participate, something that had not been encouraged in the past.

In some respects, the story of the pubs of Ireland is one of the decline of a historically important public institution that happens to be a for-profit business. However, it is also the story of entrepreneurial pub owners, some of whom are finding creative ways to survive, and a national government that seems to be awakening to the economic and social value of these enterprises. However it is perceived, this case certainly demonstrates how context (economic, political, and social) shapes entrepreneurial activity and vice versa.

The last two cases, found in Chapter 10, examine the role of entrepreneurship in revitalizing indigenous communities. As is true of all of these cases, they demonstrate how markets and entrepreneurship can be used to address social challenges, including wealth inequality. In Arizona, youth entrepreneurship is emphasized as a means of demonstrating the practical value of education, developing skills for economic self-reliance, and facilitating community building. In this case, the community is developing the capacity of its newest generation to be economic and social leaders. Alaska uses a business structure, the Alaska Native Corporation, to guide the governance, community, and economic development of its indigenous people. This makes the entire community a social enterprise and the melding of business and community virtually seamless.

These latter two cases provide an interesting counterpoint to the more Western cultural orientation of this book, which comes from the perspective that society needs to reframe its thinking about business from an individual to a community endeavor—that entrepreneurship can benefit individuals, families, *and* entire communities. These cases demonstrate that this is possible. The question is whether it is possible only because of the orientation of indigenous culture or if it can be transferred to other types of communities. The ultimate lesson here may well be that while the idea that wealth inequality can be addressed through entrepreneurship may be universal, the way in which that is manifested must be culturally specific. Context matters, and some communities may be better positioned to be socially entrepreneurial than others.

Common Themes

While each of the cases presented are unique in certain ways, there are crosscutting themes that are helpful to our understanding of how entrepreneurship might be used as a tool for mitigating wealth inequality. We catalog these themes and offer the following observations:

–   *There are many ways to address wealth inequality through entrepreneurship.* As is the case in most situations, there is more than one solution to a problem. The cases explored in this book are representative of a diversity of solutions. There is variation by the creativity of the social entrepreneurs implementing the solution, by the nature and organization of the social entrepreneurs themselves, and by the community context.

–   *The crucial need for intentionality.* In all of these cases, a community or an entrepreneurial organization had to take a leadership role and intentionally address the problem. Wealth inequality has thrived when traditional markets are allowed to follow their natural course. Markets are flawed and tend to create "winners" and "losers," as individuals pursue their own economic rationality. Fortunately, the field of behavioral economics informs us that people are not always economically rational (Kahneman & Tversky, 1984). They will depart from that which is best for them economically in order to invest in something that is better for society. This is what this sample of communities and organizations has done.

–   *The blending of business sensibility and social sensitivity.* At the core of all the efforts examined in these cases is the belief that a business entrepreneurship approach can be used effectively to accomplish a social mission. In part, this is about using markets responsibly; however, it is also about understanding and accepting that entrepreneurship is a tool for creating wealth and, if used broadly, can distribute the opportunity for wealth creation to more individuals and families. As noted earlier in this chapter, getting to the place where business and society are intermingled seamlessly can be easier in some cultures than it is in others. Traditional Western culture places the individual above the community. For people immersed in this culture, business is an individual pursuit, pitting individuals against each other in competition. For indigenous groups in the United States, the community comes before the individual. In this latter culture, business is pursued for the benefit of the community. Yet, harnessing entrepreneurship for combatting wealth inequality is not asking either culture to abandon its beliefs. When social entrepreneurship abets commercial entrepreneurship to improve the lives of community residents, we have the meeting and merging of these two worlds.

- *A broad definition of "entrepreneurship."* While a few of our examples may have limited their support of entrepreneurship to members of the community or to certain economic sectors, most followed a "big tent" policy when it came to the entrepreneurs they supported. Even those that limited their assistance to community members accepted all types of businesses, and those that focused on certain industries did not discriminate by size of business or skill level of the entrepreneur.
- *The value of intersectoral partnerships.* Architects of several of these various efforts to encourage entrepreneurship for the benefit of the community have recognized the complexity of such an endeavor and have brought together partners representing the key sectors of that community. The recognition that one perspective and one skill set are insufficient to the task is crucial to success.
- *Assistance with the intent of fostering independence.* The social entrepreneurs in these cases were not operating charities or traditional social service agencies, which too often breed dependency. They were empowering people to be more independent through successful business ownership. In many cases, intentionally or not, the social entrepreneurs were role modeling entrepreneurial thinking and behavior to the entrepreneurs they were assisting.

Limitations of These Approaches

These cases are thought provoking, and in some instances inspiring, examples of how people across the United States and elsewhere are using entrepreneurship to mitigate wealth inequality. Yet, they have their limitations. Each represents an essential step on the way but, in and of itself, is insufficient to the task.

To fully understand why this is the case requires thinking about the ultimate goal of an effort to address the significantly uneven distribution of wealth in a society through entrepreneurship. What is ultimately desired is the transformation of the society's economy from its current state to one in which the opportunity to build wealth is widespread, and support for those who wish to pursue this opportunity is permanent and equally available to all. Effecting a transformation such as this requires being intentional about undertaking change, systemic in thinking, strategic in design, and systematic in implementation. In short, it requires a large and significant commitment of political will, time, and resources.

The first inclination in pursuing this kind of transformation is to use a top-down, command and control approach. It is believed by many that this is the only way to get people in line to do what needs to be done. However, this is short-sighted and efforts that pursue this approach, in whatever form, have historically proven to be ineffective in the long run. Think about the major technological innovations, like eBay and Facebook, which have revolutionized the way people interact economically and socially. They are admittedly flawed and steadily evolving, but they have created platforms that systemically guide human activity in which engagement is horizontal and voluntary. They demonstrate that it is possible to *guide* desired human behavior without forcing it.

An entrepreneurship-based approach lends itself particularly well to transforming wealth creation because it is not suggesting the overthrow of capitalism or the abandonment of free choice. It is employing markets and expanding opportunity to all who are properly motivated to participate. It merely insists upon capitalism that is practiced responsibly, with attention to the wellbeing of the community and society. It is *both* bottom-up in that it is driven by local needs *and* top-down in the sense that it is systemic in approach, being governed by a confederation of the stakeholders involved.

There are several inter-related reasons that not one of the cases explored in this book can achieve the transformation just described. First, with the possible exception of the MSU Product Center, each program lacks the necessary comprehensiveness. There are key stakeholder groups that are missing from these programs. An otherwise promising effort at the Westside Xcelerator failed because the context-based needs of the entrepreneurs being assisted were not considered, which resulted in the exclusion of groups in the community that could have helped with addressing these needs. A complete system of support was not created. In several of the cases, local efforts were not well connected to the global economy, causing pressures from the latter to buffet and challenge the local program. Even the Product Center, which has built its networks to foster comprehensiveness, has not completely succeeded in achieving exhaustiveness in its support for its clients. More could be done to ensure its stability and permanence through the creation of additional and stronger partnerships and alliances.

By themselves, none of the example programs is capable of achieving the scale of impact necessary to transform the economy through their entrepreneurship support efforts. Arguably, each of these programs is doing its part to improve the quality of entrepreneurship in its community; however, the quantity of entrepreneurs receiving support is insufficient. This is an impossible task for a single program or organization. Each, though, would make an excellent component of a larger system of entrepreneurship support.

Some of the programs examined were pilots—Competition THRIVE and the Warsaw Entrepreneurship Forum most notably—that have not yet been adopted as permanent institutions of support and may never be. However, permanence or consistency of support over time is crucial to successful entrepreneur development, which is a long game, not a short-term economic fix. Competition THRIVE is a good example of how political shifts can disrupt and ultimately destroy an otherwise effective program and why government may not be the best leader of entrepreneurship support efforts. The THRIVE pilot lasted for three years. It was created under one New York City mayoral administration and operated for two years. A new administration was elected to office just before the third year of the program was to commence. This administration decided to keep THRIVE for one more year and then shifted its resources to another initiative. While the legacy of THRIVE lives on in the increased capability of the ESOs it touched, there will be no expansion of these efforts. The Warsaw Entrepreneurship Forum created a similar legacy in one of the six districts of Warsaw it affected because the program shrank dramatically when the European Union money that funded it dried up. Unless, or until, an entrepreneurship support effort is institutionalized, it will be vulnerable to political and budgetary exigencies.

Another limitation of the approaches represented in the case studies is that, with the exception of Competition THRIVE, none of these programs included an effort to develop the capability of the social entrepreneurs whose work is crucial to the successful development of the skills of commercial entrepreneurs. The focus is typically on the commercial entrepreneurs, themselves. There is nothing inherently wrong with this, but for a transformational system to be built, attention must be paid to its key human infrastructure and enhancing their skillset and their capacity to work collaboratively with other social entrepreneurs and enterprises.

Finally, the limitations noted above speak to one over-riding shortcoming of the cases in this book. They are all transactional in nature. They are all programs that involve relatively short-term, arm's length relationships. They are not built to achieve the kind of economic transformation being sought. Transactional relationships are sufficient for business. It is very efficient to exchange $2 for a loaf of bread. If this happens many times, the bread seller can earn a healthy profit. However, transformation involves deep, lasting change. It is about development as well as growth. It is the highest order economic offering and the least understood (Pine & Gilmore, 1999). It can only be achieved through the synergy created by being systemic, which brings us back to the original concept in this section of the chapter. It also begs the question, "What kind of system *should* we be creating?"

The Ecosystem Approach

The effort to mitigate wealth inequality through entrepreneurship needs to be scaled to include the entire community or region and all the relevant social enterprises necessary to developing successful entrepreneurs. These players must be better prepared to play their roles effectively, and they must be woven into a network of support that is transparent to entrepreneurs and prospective entrepreneurs. Such networks are being called "entrepreneurial ecosystems."

Entrepreneurial ecosystems (EEs) have been described as "inter-connected collections of actors, institutions, social structures, and cultural values that produce entrepreneurial activity" (Roundy, 2017: 1252). Like their namesakes from ecology, EEs comprise a community of symbiotic players and their support infrastructure. They have become a very "hot" topic in the economic development world because of the success of a number of them in spurring innovation and generating jobs through the efforts of the entrepreneurs they support (think the Silicon Valley).

To date, most of the attention of scholars of EEs has been directed toward their essential components or elements. Isenberg (2011) identifies six major "domains" of an EE:
- Financial capital
- Human capital
- A supportive culture
- A variety of supporting institutions and infrastructure
- Leadership and policies that sustain
- Markets for the products of the enterprises in the ecosystem

Spigel and Harrison (2017) observe three key elements of these ecosystems: cultural (positive and negative attitudes toward entrepreneurship); social (financial capital, human capital; and entrepreneurial knowledge delivered through social networks); and material (physical resources, government programs, universities, and ESOs). Autio et al. (2018) describe the essential components of an EE as being a platform that employs the advantages of digital technology to support the complex interactions of multiple players and a set of advantages created by spatial proximity.

While the makeup of an EE is important, the nature of the interactions among the elements is crucial to success. Goal attainment is less attributable to the *availability* of resources than it is to their *accessibility* to entrepreneurs. Both a rich collection of resources and a strong set of social networks through which these resources flow to the entrepreneurs who need them characterize robust EEs. Figure 11.1 attempts to capture the essence of this thinking. We would take this a step further and assert that a strong EE moreover prepares entrepreneurs to *use* available and accessible resources. It should not be assumed that entrepreneurs are capable of effectively managing the resources they have. This requires appropriate skills (Lichtenstein & Lyons, 2010). It also is useful to think of an EE as an ongoing process that reproduces and transforms itself (Spigel & Harrison, 2017). It is more a living organism than it is an enterprise-creating machine.

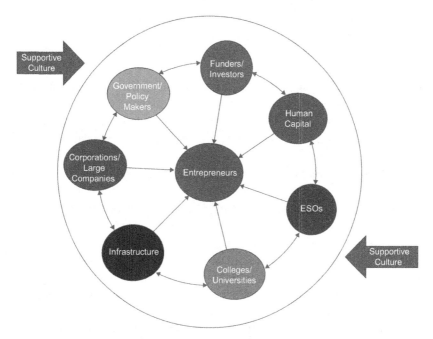

Figure 11.1: The Essence of an Entrepreneurial Ecosystem

The purpose of EEs is still open to debate. Most people who study this phenomenon describe it as focusing on high-growth, entrepreneurial ventures. This is viewed as an improvement over regional economic development efforts that strive to support all entrepreneurial activity because high-growth ventures have the greatest beneficial impact on the economy. It has even been asserted that such EEs facilitate the effort to "pick winners" in the attempt by economic developers to encourage the most impactful entrepreneurship (Spigel & Harrison, 2017: 153; Cukier et al., 2016; Storey, 2005). However, some scholars argue that because the chief purpose of EEs is to advance the economy and thereby the quality of life in a region, they have a social mission. Spigel & Harrison (2017: 164), discussing the work of Stam (2015), assert that EEs "...must be designed with an eye toward increasing the overall prosperity of a place rather than furthering regional inequality." Others, who argue that a diversity of types of entrepreneurs is beneficial to the social goals of EEs because it supports the work of social entrepreneurs and vice versa (Roundy, 2017), have further advanced this line of reasoning.

We would contend that, when it comes to mitigating wealth inequality, the best design for an EE incorporates both of these approaches. While a strict adherence to a policy of picking winners among entrepreneurs and enterprises may itself prove elitist and counterproductive, it is essential that the operating definition of "entrepreneurship" include a goal of growth on the part of the entrepreneur. This is how wealth is built. Thus, an EE with a social mission of addressing wealth inequality will wisely focus its resources on growth-oriented entrepreneurs, as opposed to "mom and pop" operators, and other forms of self-employment, where growth is not the objective. Having said this, the approach of such an EE should be to create an ecosystem that supports the development of *all* entrepreneurs who are innovating and pursuing growth. In this way, the EE is not striving to pick winners but to create an environment in which more winners are created. This dovetails well with the broadly observed phenomena among EEs that they are distinguished by being agnostic as to the industry of the resident entrepreneurs and noncompetitive (Autio et al., 2018; Spigel & Harrison, 2017).

Circling back to the elements of an effective EE, one component that is universally noted is culture. This refers to the general attitude of the community or region toward entrepreneurship. Is it understood? Are the contributions of entrepreneurs to the economy and quality of life known and appreciated? Is entrepreneurship equated with greed, as it is in some religious communities? Do people embrace thinking and acting like an entrepreneur as being desirable and important life skills? Some scholars of EEs contend that it is difficult to create an entrepreneurial culture where one did not previously exist, particularly through some form of outside intervention (Spigel & Harrison, 2017). While we would agree that it is difficult, it is not impossible, and it is essential work in those communities that have lapsed into dependency because of their history with dominant corporate, governmental or other institutions. All communities started out their history as entrepreneurial. Some unlearned such skills and now need to relearn those (Lichtenstein & Lyons, 2010).

One other major consideration that must be taken into account when examining EEs is governance. How should these large, complex systems be managed? There is surprisingly very little treatment of this important subject in the EE research literature. Now, the consensus seems to be that these systems need to be led by business or social entrepreneurs, themselves, and not government. Government should play a facilitative role, instead (Spigel & Harrison, 2017; Stam, 2015; Lerner, 2009). This tends to support one of the lessons learned in the Warsaw Entrepreneurship Forum case. This approach makes sense from a practical standpoint as well, as entrepreneurs tend to trust and respect other entrepreneurs most. Systems, the success of which rely on social capital building, would benefit from the trust that an entrepreneur(s) in the leadership role would bring.

What does all of this suggest for an entrepreneurial ecosystem the mission of which is to address wealth inequality? First, entrepreneurs, and more to the point social entrepreneurs, should lead it. They can be trusted to uphold the mission. Government should play a facilitative role; however, it should not be assumed that this institution automatically will know how best to do this. They will need to be prepared for this role by the social entrepreneurial leadership. Both the entrepreneurial landscape and the material resources of the region will need to be mapped. The social networking essential to the productive flow of resources then can be facilitated.

In most cases, the cultural element will need to be developed or, more accurately, redeveloped. There are very few "naturally entrepreneurial" regions in existence these days. A frame will be needed for preparing entrepreneurs to use resources and engage in social networks. Doing all of this effectively involves the integration of two crucial functions: (1) preparing the community to think and act entrepreneurially in support of the efforts of local entrepreneurs and (2) creating a broadly accessible system for developing properly motivated individuals into successful entrepreneurs (Markley et al., 2015). Arguably, one of the most successful approaches to carrying out the first of these two functions is that of the Center for Rural Entrepreneurship (CRE) headquartered in Lincoln, Nebraska. While this group has been rural focused, their Energizing Entrepreneurs (E^2) model is equally applicable to urban communities, and, in fact, they have been approached with increased frequency by the latter to lend their help. CRE bases its work on three fundamental principles:
- Entrepreneurship is a central strategy for all community economic development efforts.
- If a community is to become entrepreneurial, this must start with a change in culture.
- Collaboration and a systemic approach are key to a successful entrepreneurial community.

E^2 is a framework for helping the civic and business leadership of a given community to develop an appropriate mindset, leadership capabilities, and the capacity to engage in continuous learning and innovation—in other words, to become civic or social entrepreneurs (Markley et al., 2015).

The second crucial function necessary to creating a wealth-building entrepreneurial ecosystem is a system for developing the skills of the community's commercial entrepreneurs. Elsewhere, we have advocated for such a system that is available to all entrepreneurs and prospective entrepreneurs who are sufficiently motivated to do the work necessary to skill development. We envision this system as assessing individual entrepreneurs' current skills in a clinical way and using the results of this assessment to inform the work of coaches, who both provide guidance and refer entrepreneurs to appropriate support organizations for business, financial, and technical assistance (Lichtenstein & Lyons, 2010; Markley et al., 2015; Lyons & Lyons, 2015).

These two systems—the one for building community capacity in support of entrepreneurship and the one for developing the entrepreneurs, themselves—must be fully integrated (Markley et al., 2015). In this ecosystem, the social entrepreneurs of the community are constantly innovating in the ways they create the assets and infrastructure necessary to fostering community wealth creation through the successful efforts of the commercial entrepreneurs.

It should also be noted at this point that the system for developing entrepreneurs can, and should, support the activities of individual social entrepreneurs and their enterprises that are delivering social goods and services to the community. The innovative solutions these social entrepreneurs bring to such societal problems as a lack of affordable housing, insufficient childcare, poor quality education, and substance abuse, among others help to increase the community's capacity for wealth creation, something that would have been useful to the efforts of the Westside Xcelerator. Thinking has already begun regarding the tailoring of community enterprise development efforts to meet the needs of these social entrepreneurs (Lyons & Lichtenstein, 2010; Kickul & Lyons, 2016). As Roundy (2017) has noted, having these social entrepreneurs in the ecosystem can add productive diversity and heighten the attractiveness of the system as well.

Positive Signs Going Forward

The growing interest in entrepreneurial ecosystems by both scholars and practitioners is encouraging. The more we know about what works and why, the stronger efforts to support entrepreneurship on a community- or region-wide basis will be. While it is true that much of this interest is still focused on high technology entrepreneurship, there are signs that interest is growing in ecosystems with a social mission.

In a chapter in the *Handbook of Research on Social Entrepreneurship*, Lyons and Lichtenstein (2010) discuss the application of their "pipeline of entrepreneurs and enterprises" model, which is discussed in Chapter 4 of this book and depicted in Figure 4.1, to a system for fostering social entrepreneurship. They adapt both the required skills and the stages in the business life cycle to reflect the realities of social enterprise. In effect, they are providing a tool for the management of a mission-based entrepreneurial ecosystem, the mission of which could be the mitigation of wealth inequality.

Thomsen et al. (2018) explore university-based social entrepreneurship ecosystems and their role in supporting social enterprise by leveraging adult learning theory. Stam (2015) develops a framework for examining the elements of entrepreneurial ecosystems and their interactions in aid of regional entrepreneurship policy. An ecosystem for social entrepreneurs in the Seattle, Washington area is examined by Thompson et al. (2018), who conclude that such ecosystems are created through the coalescence of individuals and groups within the community and not an outside force, such as government. Ariza-Montes and Muniz (2013) argue for virtual ecosystems that have the power to generate innovation and speed the scaling of social ventures. Finally, Kickul and Lyons (2016) include a chapter on "social entrepreneurship support ecosystems" in their textbook on social entrepreneurship. All of this work improves our understanding of the ecosystem approach as a means to supporting entrepreneurship with a purpose—entrepreneurship that intentionally addresses wealth inequality—and disperses that knowledge more widely.

It helps their sustainability when entrepreneurial ecosystems are understood by, and have the broad support of, people in the community or region in which they are formed. With this in mind, another positive sign for the future is the growing economic and political power and influence of the so-called Millennial Generation. This group is broadly defined as the generation born after 1980 and into the early 2000s. They are known for their desire to make a difference in the world and for their propensity to forge strong social ties among themselves. Unlike prior generations, they generally have not known job security, affordable healthcare, or cradle-to-grave benefits of any kind. They face an uncertain economic future. As a result, they are a very entrepreneurial generation. Because they are not entitled, they have not become mired in anger about their economic lot, expecting someone else to "fix" things for them. They create their own businesses. Many of them actively support social causes, and some have become social entrepreneurs. Arguably, more than any generation, they appreciate the power of entrepreneurship and the value of collective efforts that support it.

Conclusion

Entrepreneurship, both commercial and social, can be the vehicle for providing market-based solutions to the challenges of wealth inequality. The activities of the commercial entrepreneurs of these communities can generate wealth for them, their families and the community. This will not necessarily happen, however, unless these entrepreneurs are supported in their development by the community and are connected to the larger economy.

Government, nonprofit and for-profit entities, acting as social entrepreneurs, as in the examples offered in this book, can provide this support. In order to achieve success in this endeavor; however, these entities must move beyond fragmented, programmatic responses to systemic approaches that connect them into a seamless support ecosystem that is transparent to the entrepreneurs they are seeking to serve. This will yield the synergies necessary to the economic, and ultimately social, transformation of the community. This is the kind of responsible capitalism that can help to address wealth inequality and the marginalization of lower-income communities.

References

Ariza-Montes, J.A., & Muniz, N.M. (2013). Virtual ecosystems in social business incubation. *Journal of Electronic Commerce in Organizations* 11 (3): 27.

Autio, E., Nambisan, S., Thomas, L.D.W., & Wright, M. (2018). Digital affordances, spatial affordances, and the genesis of entrepreneurial ecosystems. *Strategic Entrepreneurship Journal* 12: 72–95.

Cukier, D., Kon, F., & Lyons, T.S. (2016). 22nd ICE/IEEE International Technology Management Conference, Trondheim, Norway, "Software Startup Ecosystems: The New York City Case Study," June 13–15.

Kahneman, D., & Tversky, A. (1984). Choices, values and frames. *American Psychologist* 39 (4): 341–350.

Kickul, J., & Lyons, T.S. (2016). *Understanding social entrepreneurship: The relentless pursuit of mission in an ever changing world.* New York: Routledge.

Lerner, J. (2009). *Boulevard of broken dreams: Why public efforts to boost entrepreneurship and venture capital have failed and what to do about it.* Princeton, NJ: Princeton University Press.

Lichtenstein, G.A., & Lyons, T.S. (2010). *Investing in entrepreneurs: A strategic approach for strengthening your regional and community economy.* Santa Barbara, CA: Praeger/ABC-CLIO.

Lyons, T.S., & Lichtenstein, G.A., (2010). A community-wide framework for encouraging social entrepreneurship using the pipeline of entrepreneurs and enterprises model. In Fayolle, A. & Matlay, H. *Handbook of research on social entrepreneurship.* Cheltenham, UK: Edward Elgar.

Lyons, T.S., & Lyons, J.S. (2015). A skills assessment approach for operationalizing entrepreneur skill theory. White paper. Morristown, NJ: LEAP LLC.

Macke, D. (2018) Is entrepreneurship a pathway to greater wealth equality? Retrieved from https://www.energizingentrepreneurs.org. Accessed June 20, 2018.

Markley, D.M., Lyons, T.S., & Macke, D.W. (2015). Creating entrepreneurial communities: Building community capacity for ecosystem development. *Community Development* 46 (5): 580--598.

Neck, H.M., Neck, C.P., & Murray, E.L. (2018). *Entrepreneurship: The practice and the mindset.* Los Angeles, CA: Sage.

Pine, B.J., II, & Gilmore, J.H. (1999). *The experience economy.* Boston, MA: Harvard Business School Press.

Roundy, P.T. (2017). Social entrepreneurship and entrepreneurial ecosystems: Complementary or disjoint phenomena. *International Journal of Social Economics* 44 (9): 1252–1267.

Spigel, B., & Harrison, R. (2017). Toward a process theory of entrepreneurial ecosystems. *Strategic Entrepreneurship Journal* 12: 151–168.

Stam, E. (2015). Entrepreneurial ecosystems and regional policy: A sympathetic critique. *European Planning Studies* 23 (9), 1759–1769.

Storey, D.J. (2005). Entrepreneurship, small and medium sized enterprises and public policies. In Z.J. Acs & D.B. Audretsch (Eds.). *Handbook of entrepreneurship research* (pp. 473–511). Cheltenham, UK: Edward Elgar.

Thompson, T.A., Purdy, J.M., Ventresca, M.J. (2018). How entrepreneurial ecosystems take form: Evidence from social impact initiatives in Seattle. *Strategic Entrepreneurship Journal* 12 (1): 96–116.

Thomsen, B., Olav, M., & Best, T. (2018). The political ecology of university-based social entrepreneurship ecosystems. *Journal of Enterprising Communities* 12 (2): 199–219.

Index

DOI 10.1515/9781547400461-012

Made in the USA
Coppell, TX
16 January 2020